OCCUPATION LIFE

Real Lives on
German Occupied Guernsey

by
Molly Bihet

For Jess,
With my best Wishes,
Molly Bihet.
22nd June 2014.
Guernsey.

printed
printedinguernsey.com

OCCUPATION LIFE
Real Lives on German Occupied Guernsey

First published: October 2014
© *Molly Bihet*
All rights reserved.

British Library Cataloguing in Publication Data.

A catalogue record for this book is available from the British Library.

ISBN: 978-0-9510619-8-5

Printed by: Printed, Guernsey.

Copies of OCCUPATION LIFE are available from all good Guernsey bookshops or by post from:-

Molly Bihet, Rose-Adele, Les Amballes, St Peter Port, Guernsey GY1 1WY. Other books available from Molly include A Child's War, Reflections of Guernsey and A Time for Memories.

Dedicated to my two lovely daughters and our grandchildren of whom I am very proud. May they always enjoy peace and freedom.

Thanks and Acknowledgements

My sincere thanks, especially to my family, who have helped in many ways (with patience) with the creation of this book. I am also grateful to friends, particularly Simon Hamon for scanning and providing several of the photographs. To Sarah and Jon Taylor for placing photographs and typesetting the book. Thanks also to Malcolm and Pam Woodland for their efforts in helping with the research. To Stan Bichard, Renaut de Garis, for his story, Michael Williams, John Goodwin, Marion Jones, Roy Falla, Jean Sargent, David Pattimore, Richard Heaume, Graham Williams, Ken Tough, Yvonne Fisher, Paul Upton, Jim Priaulx, Hilmar and Regina Schope-Hellwig, Peter de Sausmarez, Mary Sims, Milton Brehaut, John Williams, Mac McDonald, Tim & Emma Feak and Brenda Bailey.

Thanks also to The Channel Island Occupation Society, The Guernsey Press & Star, The Priaulx Library, The Island Archives and The Royal Court Library. Special thanks go to Anna Packham and Tom Peek at Printed.

My appreciation and special thanks, also go to Dame Mary Perkins for writing the Foreword.

Foreword

Molly Bihet brings to life completely as to how the occupation of Guernsey on 30th June 1940 affected the lives of those left behind.

Every parent, reading Molly's memories in "OCCUPATION LIFE Real Lives on German Occupied Guernsey", can relate to the agonising decisions as to whether their young children should be evacuated or not. All those feelings come through vividly.

Each chapter introduces us to a colourful Guernsey man or woman, and how they coped with living daily struggles to get food, heating and everything that was taken for granted previously, such as being able to wash with soap.

At the same time, Molly brings out the humour which, undoubtedly, helped everyone to keep their spirts up. She brings a child's view of what it was like not to be evacuated, and how she saw the occupiers – some of whom were best kept clear of and others who obviously were missing their families back in Germany.

Her account of the deprivation of even basic foods, such as bread, was moving and the arrival of the Red Cross ship Vega was emotional for the reader. Most of all, Molly's words show how everyone pulled together, neighbours, friends and particularly the teachers who did their utmost to make sure the children were educated and fed.

It was a privilege to see the accompanying photographs, illustrations and documents. Guernsey should continue to be proud of those who held together so well during the occupation and those who are still here to recount their experiences for future generations. There will always be Liberation Day celebrations on 9th May every year – emotional for all of us, but especially for those with first hand memories of this so important date.

Thank you Molly.

by Dame Mary Perkins, Guernsey 2014

Contents

About the Author	9
Setting the Scene	12
The Evacuation	14
Air Raid and "They've Landed"	24
The Collins Family	31
BBC's History of the World	33
Les Côtils and Castle Carey	35
1941 – 1942 A Near Miss	39
La Vallette and Alderney: Clothes Gathered from the Sea	44
Law and Orders: Grandpa fooled the Germans	48
More Hidden Treasures: Wireless Sets	51
Vauvert School and Logbook	54
Hautes Capelles School, St Sampson	63
Malcolm Woodland, Stan & Leslie Bichard	68
Food 1941-42	72
Games which annoyed Otto and Hamel	80
Entertainment: The Finigan Sisters	84
Threats and Deportation	89
Internment and Deportation 'G.U.N.S.' 1942-1943	94
Two Brave Women Imprisoned	100
Intermediate School	104
Diary of a Night-time Central Telephone Operator	112
Renaut de Garis and The Mirus Battery	119
Rationing 1944: Food & Heating	125
The Red Cross Saved Lives	131
Hungry German Soldiers at our Dustbins	140
Liberation	142
Freddie Frinton came for Tea	150
After Liberation and Force 135	153
The Victory Parade, London 1946	157
Co-incidences 1940, 1980 & 2011	159
Dinner for One!	164
Looking Back	168

About the Author

I was born in 1931 to parents Gladys ("Glad" née Collins) and William (Bill) Finigan. My parents and myself have always lived and were born in St Peter Port, the main town of Guernsey. Not one of us have ever wanted to live anywhere else! Mum and Dad started married life at 6am in St Joseph's Church on the 28th December 1926 by special licence. They lived in a very small flat over the Guernsey Dairy in Havilland Street. When I was a toddler, we moved into a small cottage (one of three situated around a courtyard) into the next road, St John's Street. My grandmother died in 1939, so the family moved again to be with my grandfather at Rose Villa, 30 Les Canichers, of which I have very vivid and clear memories.

At this time I was 8 years old, and my sister Joyce was 6 years old. I expect we were sorry to leave our young friends at the courtyard as we had a very happy childhood with them there. I remember our nice neighbours very well, but not so nice were the neighbours who arrived in 1940! I left school at 14 and began working in the office at the Central Telephone Exchange and worked there for almost 10 years.

I married André in 1954. He was also born in St Peter Port, although his parents were French (hence the name Bihet). I never thought at any age, I would be writing of the Occupation for a book, but I began in 1985 when all the islands were going to celebrate the anniversary of 40 years of freedom. After Dad died in 1972, Mum left the family home at Rose Villa (number 30) and came to live with us and our two daughters at Woodcote, which was situated opposite Rose Villa. We were running a successful and friendly guest house and spent many happy and amusing evenings with my mother telling the guests her Occupation stories. The visitors all thought my mother should write a book about it but at her age she was just happy to tell the stories to make people laugh, although it was not funny at the time I can assure you. Hence the writing was left to me, as my husband encouraged me to write and have our family stories printed. The timing was certainly right as I received so many grateful letters and thanks for writing, especially of my mother and grandfather! Sadly, my father never knew the success I had in writing about his and Mum's life during that time.

Mum and Grandpa

After my first book A Child's War, readers wanted to hear more about what followed Liberation, so I wrote "Reflections of Guernsey". I thought I had completed my writing, but I wanted to raise money for the British Red Cross, so I decided on a third book in 2004, entitled "A Time for Memories". I focused more on the Red Cross letters that were sent to and fro between

Channel Islanders and family and friends in the UK, and the lifesaving food parcels from the Red Cross ship SS Vega, I also appreciated being given permission to print Dame Hathaway's personal memories of Sark's Occupation. All profits from this book were sent to the British Red Cross.

Sadly, my dear husband died in November 2010 and since that time, I have received so much encouragement from islanders and readers alike, to write again. With my pride and interest in Guernsey's past, I have enjoyed the writing but I feel this could be my final effort. Although I have shortened main details of A Child's War, I hope you will forgive me for mentioning them again, and that you will still find other memories of interest, especially of the children at school and at play.

Enjoy the read.

À la perchoine, until we meet again,

SARNIA CHERIE

Molly Bihet

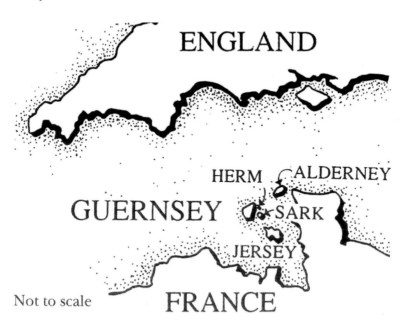

Setting the scene

The Channel Islands lie between within the English Channel and are situated much closer to France than to England. There are times on a clear day one can see the coast of Normandy on the horizon. Jersey is the largest of the Islands and the Bailiwick of Guernsey consists of Guernsey (6x4 miles), Alderney, Sark, Herm, Jethou, and all are different in character. The total area for all the Channel Islands is seventy-five square miles.

When coming and entering Guernsey's main harbour by boat, St Peter Port harbour and the town is a wonderful sight, especially at sunrise with the backdrop of the hills beyond, and many special buildings on the skyline. At any time I feel there can be no better view anywhere, especially with the high tides we get. Twice a day the tides flood the shallows around the islands and during the spring tides the rise can be as much as 10 metres (almost 40 feet). There are times when the sea level will flow across the sea front at the marina and shops, restaurants are always wise to place sand-bags for protection. The West coast too gets a battering from time to time.

During 1939 when war was declared and during 1940, the Channel Islands were still advertising the islands as a holiday destination and no-one could have foreseen what the future held. The majority thought war would not affect the islands too much, and never dreamt that Guernsey would have thousands of unwelcome guests arrive, in unusual uniforms, large helmets and heavy boots, and carrying an assortment of weapons.

Guernsey's main industry then was dairy farming, growing, fishing and tourists. Many tons of tomatoes were grown and exported every year. It was an island of some 40,000 hardworking and contented people who knew almost everyone within their own parishes. There are ten in all that make up the Island.

My memories began when I was eight, my sister was six and we were a very ordinary happy family living in a pleasant house overlooking the beautiful harbour of St. Peter Port. I remember the talk of the 'war' but it did not mean much to girls of my age. I was just old enough to knit socks and helmets at school and to bring my knitting home, all for the men going to the front.

In 1939, my mother, father and we girls had just moved to Rose Villa, Les Canichers because my grandmother had recently died so Mum and Dad decided to move and look after my grandfather (my mother's dad 'Pop Collins') and also her brother Reg, who was a semi-invalid, because he had been severely injured in the First World War 1914 – 1918.

I knew my mother and father were worried about the war and there was much talk among the grown-ups. Dad was of 'call up' age and we wondered whether he would have to leave us to go and fight.

On 16 June 1940, the small military garrison that was stationed at Castle Cornet left the Island. Talk amongst the older people was that men would be made to leave the Island to join the forces but this did not happen, although many hundreds did go straight away voluntarily to fight.

Then later in June 1940, the island authorities were concerned as the German forces had occupied Paris (France) and were overcoming towns and travelling towards the west coast just across the water from the Channel Islands. Alarm bells rang louder when six boat loads of French refugees arrived in Guernsey. They reported that their hometown of Cherbourg had been practically razed to the ground, the civilian population had fled, and fires were blazing everywhere. They also told of the terrible atrocities and brutalities that were happening on the continent. All this was on everyone's minds should the German Army decide to come here.

The Evacuation

19 June 1940 – Evacuation of children: "ALL PARENTS MUST REPORT THIS EVENING"

One can imagine how this headline news would affect everyone, especially parents and every family. It made near panic amongst the population as no-one knew what to do, nor could they decide quickly. So many good reasons why so many really wanted to stay as a family, but with thoughts of German occupation and what the French refugees had told about Cherbourg, many were frightened for their children, themselves and their homes. Just like Mum and Dad were. The situation was made worse as posters were displayed, such as "There's no place like home", "Don't be yellow – STAY!" and "Compulsory evacuation a lie!" What a dilemma for my mother, father and everyone. My Mother decided to try and travel with my sister and I and go as a helper and I can well remember leaving home around 6am with gas masks around our necks, some small carrier bags with small items of clothing and some cash carefully hidden - sewn inside our vests. "Just in case", said Mum, but three times we returned home as my mother was not allowed to travel with the school teachers and children, the latter had priority. If Mum had permitted us to leave without her, she must have felt in her heart that Joyce and I would have had to separate as we were attending different schools at the time. She must have kept hoping that the next time could see us being allowed to travel together. Yet again we tried, each time I wanted to stay with my father, my sister was crying wanting to go on the big boat and my mother I'm sure was very concerned and confused. No wonder my mother did not want to be parted from us, we were only 6 and 8 years old.

No. 10,962   REGISTERED AT THE G.P.O.   GUERNSEY, WEDNESDAY, JUNE 19, 1940   POSTAGE 1d.   TELEPHONE 1100 (FIVE LINES)   ONE PENNY

Evening Press

EVACUATION OF CHILDREN

PARENTS MUST REPORT THIS EVENING

Clothing and Ration Necessities

Arrangements are being made for the evacuation of (1) children of school age and (2) children under school age to reception areas in the United Kingdom under Government arrangement.

The evacuation is expected to take place to-morrow, the 20th June, 1940.

The mothers of children under school age will be allowed to accompany their children.

Parents of school children are to attend at the school attended by their

TO OUR READERS

From to-day the "Evening Press" will be published in its present form. Readers will appreciate that the change has been made because of the urgent necessity to economise in paper.

We are confident that readers will co-operate with us and will assist us by not obtaining additional copies unless it is essential.

A full telegraphic service and local news service will be fully maintained, as in the past.

CHERBOURG REFUGEES

SIX BOAT-LOADS ARRIVE

Guernsey first learnt of the German occupation of Cherbourg when a stream of small French craft arrived last night at St. Peter-Port from Cherbourg. They brought refugees who told how their home town had been practically razed to the ground.

The first vessel, a fishing boat, arrived at 5.30. Information was sent by German manned shore batteries and later by low-flying 'planes.

They were in excellent spirits and wanted nothing more than cigarettes and tobacco. The men, numbering 150, were commanded by Lt. Gabriel Robert. They came in the Confiance-en-Dieu, Fleur de Lisieux, both of Boulogne; La Portaix, of Caen, and Vonnette, of Gravelines. Large crowds watched their arrival in the Old Harbour.

After all possible had been done for the party they continued their voyage to France.

At this time, I remember all the talk to friends and relations "are you going?" or "are you going to stay?", "what are we going to do?" - the phone kept ringing and Mum and Dad were very worried as to what was going to happen to us all. If parents wanted their children to go to England with the school, special arrangements had to be made and they had to report at their school at a given time and be prepared ready to join the ships and leave. Some children had a long wait but had to return home again and then was given a different time to report. At Burnt Lane and St Joseph's Schools, all had to assemble at St Joseph's School - my husband André, who was twelve at the time, remembers going with his mother very early (around 4-5am) in the morning to the school, saying good-bye there, then walking down with teachers to the harbour. He remembers being lined up like all the other children in particular school groups, being checked, then getting on board. It was the talk of everyone but what a difficult decision to make. Leaving their homes probably for the first time ever, in those days in the 1930's, it was an occasion to cross the water and spend a day on "Herm" which was a 30 minute boat trip! Now the Islanders were being advised to leave their homes and cross the water for an indefinite period.

The Reason We Stayed

The reason my parents hesitated in leaving and there was so much tension and worry in our home as there were six in the family at Rose Villa. Firstly, my old Grandfather (Pop Collins as he was known and you will hear later the character he was!) was over 70 and had been born at Rose Villa and being very stubborn was definitely not going to leave his home for anyone, lease of all the Germans! As it was, all the Collins family plus Joyce and I had been born at No 30, Rose Villa, our home - my mother and her two sisters and three brothers as well. My Uncle (Reg Collins) who my mother was looking after, had been severely wounded in the First World War and had a bullet lodged in his spine for many years. He had a stiff leg and found it difficult in walking well – so he had also made up his mind, he was staying. This left my Father to decide he was running a small building business and he felt he ought to stay a little longer to sort things out and for Pop and Uncle Reg. He desperately wanted my mother to leave with us girls and catch the boat and said he would follow later – so many dads would have said the same thing but arrangements had to be made very quickly.

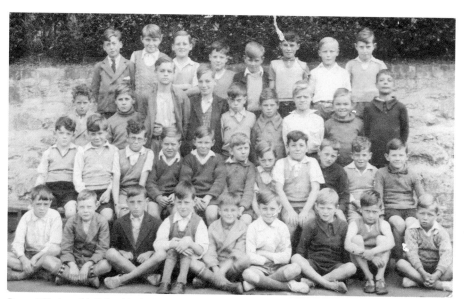

Boys at St. Joseph's School in the late 1930s. André is seated, front row, 4th from the right

KEEP YOUR HEADS!

DON'T BE YELLOW!

BUSINESS AS

USUAL

There was just no time to think straight. One cannot fully realise what everyone was feeling until one is older when having your own children and grandchildren. When giving talks to groups about the Occupation, I always say that I feel this was the worst period of our war. No-one knew what to do for the best but early next morning, boats arrived and the evacuation began. Within two to three days, almost half of Guernsey's population of 43,820 had left, including 5,000 children mostly with teachers. Approximately 1000 children stayed on the island and my sister and I were amongst them. With these numbers mostly queuing to get on the boats, I remember the crowds surrounding us each time mum tried to travel with us – but each time we returned home and I expect we were very pleased to get away from so many unhappy and tearful people and the crushing of so many. It was after the fourth attempt, the decision was made for us. We just had to stay and the evacuation just came to a complete stop.

My late husband André remembers meeting very early in the morning (before 6am) at the school with a small carrier bag containing a little lunch, a change of under-clothing and a few pence. I expect that was about it. Children were to be evacuated together as a school with some teachers willing to go and travel with them. When André arrived in Weymouth, the school group travelled by train with some of the 1300 evacuees to Glasgow in Scotland. He remembered young boys being very tearful without their parents but as he was 12 years old, he found the trip more like an adventure and most like him had never seen a moving train or even black and white cows! More boys than girls would be happy leaving, but many of the children were toddlers in their first year of school and were crying for their parents when arriving in Glasgow after such a very long journey.

Everyone was tired on arrival, and the smaller children were probably bewildered as to what was happening. Some parents were only given two hours notice to take the children to their school, ready to leave. John Williams from St Joseph's School was also with André on the Antwerp and kindly gave me a list of evacuees of children who left on the boats and more details with grateful thanks to Simon Hamon of the Occupation Society.

John also remembers seeing just before their arrival in Weymouth, a sunken ship with the stern well above the water. The boys thought it had just happened, but he later found out she was the 'British Inventor', a 7101 ton tanker who had struck a mine on the 13 June 1940, just a week previously. The ship was eventually towed into Southampton and rebuilt.

The list on page 18 is of the ships primarily involved in the evacuation from Guernsey. **20**

Guernsey evacuees arriving at the Hale Station. The boy pictured is carrying his belongings in a Guernsey chip basket.

More arrivals. (Image coutesy Simon Hamon and C.I.O.S).

Vessel	Number of Evacuees	Time/Date of Departure	School
Antwerp	1,154	20th June, 10am	St Josephs, Amherst, St Sampson
Felixstowe	437	20th June	Vauvert
Batavia	800	20th June 11:55pm	Intermediate & Colleges
Hazelmere	300	20th June 2.30pm	Vauvert and Notre Dame
Sheringham	750	21st June, 3.30am	Vale and Torteval
Viking	1,880	21st June, 7am	
Duke of York	2,000	21st June	(1000 infants and expectant mothers)

Later another 25 ships sailed with more of the civilian population from Guernsey within this short time. More details of the vast evacuation has been recorded and written by Simon Hamon in the 39th edition of the Channel Islands Occupation review. My thanks to him also to John Williams now living in the UK. What a mammoth job was done at the Guernsey harbour and also at Weymouth docks where 58 ships birthed during the 3 days of

S.S. HASELMERE built 1925 for Southern Railway, arriving at St Peter Port. (SH)

the evacuation. It is only when writing of it does the mind realise how awful it must have been for everyone.

This list proves that mum would have been correct – my sister and I would have been separated as I was at Notre Dame (Burnt Lane) and Joyce was at St Josephs – both town Catholic schools, but we would have had to travel on different boats.

She was also correct in not sending Joyce and I to her sister, Lillian, living with her family in Greenwich in London as like thousands of others endured endless bombing raids and lived underground at the railway station for many months. They too lived not knowing what the next day would bring. In many ways it was a blessing that so many children had evacuated, as all through the five years, parents were only too willing to part with their children's clothes, shoes and games etc, to help all the children who stayed. They would give, sell or exchange through the newspaper or barter shops that opened.

Families and friends still on the island were desperate for news of their loved ones, especially of their children but had to wait some four and five months and then with only a five word message through the Red Cross: a relief for so many despite such a few words. More of the Red Cross in "A Time for Memories".

On arrival in the UK, many sad stories were told of people putting their beloved pets to sleep before leaving homes, which caused so much heartache.

I had read also of old people being abandoned and left behind and of a baby being left in a shop.

One gent arrived in Bradford, told a reporter "I had just bought a house full of furniture. We were just preparing a meal when word came to leave. We left the dinner and straightaway left for the harbour". They had five children somewhere, who had already left on an earlier boat, and they didn't know where they had been taken. He was amongst the 400 who were at Bradford and told of cars just being left at the quayside. One could have bought a Rolls Royce for 10 shillings! (50p)

Another person said "We left our house just as it was. I killed the kitten and our two pet rabbits, then locked the door and pushed the key through the letter box." There were many accounts such as this, told to reporters and printed in the UK newspapers.

The teachers have since remarked that the children and grown-ups had a marvellous reception, and were looked after very well in all the towns and places they were taken to mainly to the north of the UK and Glasgow. The ages ranged from eight weeks old to the oldest of 82 years who travelled, but sadly, one child died on one of the boats.

After the vast evacuation, the following week must have been very worrying. We heard the sounds of bombardment in France, the noise of planes flying overhead, and sirens which sounded from time to time. The grown-ups were talking of reconnaissance planes (an unusual and unfamiliar word for us children) and from home we could hear the distant rumblings of warfare across the water. What with the threat of occupation and thousands of grown-ups and children having left, everyone was asking questions, "What will happen to us all? Everyone was on edge. There was one main worry, had all the children left? My mother and father just kept wondering if my sister and I were the only children left on the island, so many full boatloads of people (mostly children) had gone, could there be any families left like us? Well, thankfully there were and after the dismay and the tension of the past few days – there were friends and family still on the island. What a great relief for my parents knowing this. Come what may, we were all in the same boat so to speak.

This was the time my father and probably other men of his age, felt they should have joined up and helped the Forces. Many hundreds of islanders had joined and it was later known that 231 islanders died in the British armed forces during the war and 15 died in allied air raids.

Royal Message to the Channel Islands

BUCKINGHAM PALACE

June 24th, 1940

'For strategic reasons it has been found necessary to withdraw the armed forces from the Channel Islands. I deeply regret this necessity and I wish to assure My people in the Islands that, in taking this decision, My Government has not been unmindful of the position. It is in their interest that this step should be taken in present circumstances.

The long association of the Islands with the Crown and the loyal service that the people of the Islands have rendered to My Ancestors and Myself are guarantees that the link between us will remain unbroken and I know that My people in the Islands will look forward with the same confidence as I do to the day when the resolute fortitude with which we face our present difficulties will reap the reward of victory.'

On Monday 24th June the Bailiff received a message from his Majesty the King. One can understand difficult decisions had to be made at this time, as accompanying the King's Message was a covering letter from the home secretary to the Bailiff saying that it was a matter for the Bailiff to decide how the message should be communicated to the Islanders, *'Having regard to the interests of National Security'*. The Bailiff, while assuming wrongly that the decision of the British Government to demilitarise the Island was known to the German's, felt that the Home Secretary's letter advised caution in the publication of the King's message. He decided that the message would not be published in the newspapers, at least for the time being. Instead, he decided to read it to the small crowd assembled in Smith Street outside the Guernsey Press Office. The King's message that he read from the first floor window reached only a very small audience.

Guernsey awoke the next morning to find itself demilitarised and defenceless. Many Islanders bitterly resented being left to the mercy of the Germans.

Islanders were not helped in their decision by 'Lord Haw-Haw', William Joyce, the traitor who regulary broadcast German propaganda, sneeringly saying:

"We are coming very soon, you Channel Islanders, to get those potatoes and tomatoes. And when we've finished with you, there'll be nothing left."

The Air Raid and "They've landed"

A week later, on the lovely afternoon of 28th June, 1940 we were in the road looking out over the harbour when we heard and saw three planes come very low over the sea and harbour – we gave them a wave with a cucumber we'd just bought from a shop nearby but soon ran for shelter when we saw that the markings were German planes which started to machine-gun and bomb the ships and the harbour. We ran for shelter down some steps opposite our house and into a long corridor to the basement of a friend's house called 'Grangeclare'. There were several of us there and we were all very frightened. The harbour was so close to where we were sheltering and we had never heard anything like it before. It seemed ages before the noise of the explosions and machine gunning stopped. Eventually we came up to the road where we had originally been standing waving and we could see that there must be terrible damage as everywhere seemed to be ablaze and smoking.

Clearly we could see the extent of the air raid. There were carts and lorries burnt out, which had been loaded with tomatoes ready to be shipped to the mainland and boats bombarded. Our beautiful harbour had been transformed. Mum and Dad were very worried that Uncle Reg could be hurt or maybe killed as he was working down the harbour at the time. He eventually came home not hurt but very shocked and saddened. Thankfully, he managed to get under the jetty in time.

Having the right climate and many glasshouses (vineries), many tons of tomatoes were grown and exported as Guernsey's main industry, so it was a familiar scene at the harbour with lorries and carts queuing almost every day

Oil painting by David Le Cheminant MRCVS, depicting the bombing raid on St Peter Port Harbour
28 June 1940 *with courtesy of Malcolm Woodland*

Heinkel HE 111 medium bomber of the German Luftwaffe of the type used to bomb St Peter Port (SH)

The Harbour air raid

in a long line ready to send them away. Many, many tons of tomatoes were left to rot after the raid.

German planes thought these lorries were military vehicles holding ammunitions. They were heavily bombed and machine-gunned. Many of the drivers and workmen who were sheltering under the lorries could not get under the jetty for safety like my uncle did. They were either shot, burnt or crushed to death. The St John Ambulance was machine gunned and so was the Lifeboat on its way to Jersey, killing the coxswain's son. Bombs were dropped in other areas of the island, but damage was more severe in the Town.

The Weighbridge Clock Tower after being hit by a bomb during the air raid on St Peter Port.

Hundreds of bullet holes and shrapnel damage could be seen in the area of Le Pollet and the Royal Hotel, so very near to where we were sheltering. We were certainly frightened and the windows on the top floor of 'Grangeclare', was broken. It seemed ages listening to the explosions as the planes seemed to drop their load, but came back again with more machine gunning and explosions. The air raid lasted for over an hour and later we knew fully of the deaths and injuries the Germans had caused - 34 civilians had been killed and many injured.

The Germans had not been told that the islands had been demilitarized and were defenceless, except for one small gun on the steamer 'Isle of Sark' which was about to leave for the mainland. The three Luftwaffe pilots from the low flying aircraft came from the north, and at first I was happy to wave at them. They assumed the lorries were loaded with ammunitions, hence the onslaught, and it was yet more worry for my parents. I am sure at this time, they would have wished my sister and I anywhere other than in Guernsey – what would happen tomorrow or the next day? No-one knew, but it was a most worrying time.

It was two days later on the 30th June that news soon spread around the island quickly that the Germans had landed with no fuss at the airport. Apparently, 30 Germans arrived in five Junkers aircraft and had immediately made their presence at the Royal Hotel which was to become their main German Headquarters. It was then my mother decided to stay indoors – she did not want to face the enemy and wondered whether they were square-headed as we had heard! It was over a month later when she decided to leave the house and although still nervous decided the Germans did really look like normal human beings after all!

All communications, including postal and telephone services, with the UK was immediately stopped. At 8pm it was officially broadcast that with their arrivals, all had to behave and there was to be no talking in groups!

That was the first of the orders, but the next day and afterwards, there were many more to come.

Home Circle Library

BUSINESS AS USUAL

— AT —

Old Gate House

AND THE BRIDGE,

ST. SAMPSON'S.

Evening Press

No. 10,972   REGISTERED AT THE G.P.O. POSTAGE ½d.   · GUERNSEY, MONDAY, JULY 1, 1940   TELEPHONE 1400 (FIVE LINES)   G R A T I S

ORDERS OF THE COMMANDANT OF THE GERMAN FORCES IN OCCUPATION OF THE ISLAND OF GUERNSEY

(1)—ALL INHABITANTS MUST BE INDOORS BY 11 P.M. AND MUST NOT LEAVE THEIR HOMES BEFORE 6 A.M.

(2)—WE WILL RESPECT THE POPULATION IN GUERNSEY; BUT, SHOULD ANYONE ATTEMPT TO CAUSE THE LEAST TROUBLE, SERIOUS MEASURES WILL BE TAKEN AND THE TOWN WILL BE BOMBED.

(3)—ALL ORDERS GIVEN BY THE MILITARY AUTHORITY ARE TO BE STRICTLY OBEYED.

(4)—ALL SPIRITS MUST BE LOCKED UP IMMEDIATELY, AND NO SPIRITS MAY BE SUPPLIED, OBTAINED OR CONSUMED HENCEFORTH. THIS PROHIBITION DOES NOT APPLY TO STOCKS IN PRIVATE HOUSES.

(5)—NO PERSON SHALL ENTER THE AERODROME AT LA VILLIAZE.

(6)—ALL RIFLES, AIRGUNS, PISTOLS, REVOLVERS, DAGGERS, SPORTING GUNS, AND ALL OTHER WEAPONS WHATSOEVER, EXCEPT SOUVENIRS, MUST, TOGETHER WITH ALL AMMUNITION, BE DELIVERED AT THE ROYAL HOTEL BY 12 NOON TO-DAY, JULY 1.

(7)—ALL BRITISH SAILORS, AIRMEN AND SOLDIERS ON LEAVE IN THIS ISLAND MUST REPORT AT THE POLICE STATION AT 9 A.M. TO-DAY, AND MUST THEN REPORT AT THE ROYAL HOTEL.

(8)—NO BOAT OR VESSEL OF ANY DESCRIPTION, INCLUDING ANY FISHING BOAT, SHALL LEAVE THE HARBOURS OR ANY OTHER PLACE WHERE THE SAME IS MOORED, WITHOUT AN ORDER FROM THE MILITARY AUTHORITY, TO BE OBTAINED AT THE ROYAL HOTEL. ALL BOATS ARRIVING FROM JERSEY, FROM SARK OR FROM HERM, OR ELSEWHERE, MUST REMAIN IN HARBOUR UNTIL PERMITTED BY THE MILITARY TO LEAVE.

THE CREWS WILL REMAIN ON BOARD. THE MASTER WILL REPORT TO THE HARBOURMASTER, ST. PETER-PORT, AND WILL OBEY HIS INSTRUCTIONS.

(9)—THE SALE OF MOTOR SPIRIT IS PROHIBITED, EXCEPT FOR USE ON ESSENTIAL SERVICES, SUCH AS DOCTORS' VEHICLES, THE DELIVERY OF FOODSTUFFS, AND SANITARY SERVICES WHERE SUCH VEHICLES ARE IN POSSESSION OF A PERMIT FROM THE MILITARY AUTHORITY TO OBTAIN SUPPLIES.

THESE VEHICLES MUST BE BROUGHT TO THE ROYAL HOTEL BY 12 NOON TO-DAY TO RECEIVE THE NECESSARY PERMISSION.

THE USE OF CARS FOR PRIVATE PURPOSES IS FORBIDDEN.

(10)—THE BLACK-OUT REGULATIONS ALREADY IN FORCE MUST BE OBSERVED AS BEFORE.

(11)—BANKS AND SHOPS WILL BE OPEN AS USUAL.

(Signed) THE GERMAN COMMANDANT OF THE ISLAND OF GUERNSEY

JULY 1, 1940.

1940. We watched the parade passing the Royal Hotel on the Glategny Esplanade near our home.

The Collins family

Throughout the occupation, many laws were broken and the minor ones (such as riding two abreast on bicycles, or smoking in the cinema) would mean a fine on the spot. Others like stealing a loaf from the German store and hiding it until the coast was clear, like my cousin Sid Collins did, meant a three month prison sentence (no wonder the prison was always full). His younger brother Les was a popular Guernsey sportsman and well known footballer and boxer, even during the occupation when allowed to mix in groups. He was a real sportsman and everyone liked and knew Les Collins. One day he was working in town as a locksmith in the workshop, a German came up to him and started framing up and sparing at him. Les thought he was being friendly and thought the German had probably seen Les boxing the night before at the Regal Cinema in a bout, so Les made a jab and hit him on the nose, then hit him lower to the chest. Without thinking, Les had hit him quite hard. The German immediately went down on one knee and grunted. With that, the German got his bayonet out and Les had to dodge around a bit, and was very grateful when a German officer arrived and put a stop to it. The officer spoke perfect English and asked what was going on. It appeared the German was wanting to tell Les that he was boxing mad, that was all – but ah! It didn't stop there as two or three days later, Les was filing a key at the vice, when he heard a couple of explosions. The file Les was using flew across the bench, then his arm went limp, pouring with blood. The German had shot him in the elbow! Les had to have the bullet removed at the hospital, and he had eleven weeks at home because of the injury. He felt this episode was hushed up and nothing more was heard of this friendly sparring!

Cousin Les Collins was shot and could have been killed for sparring with a German.

Kate and William Joseph, Gran and Grandpa ('Pop'), Collins had three sons – Sidney (Sid and Les' dad), Reginald and William. Reginald Walter Francis Collins was my mother's crippled brother and 'Pop's son who I previously mentioned in 'A Child's War'. These were the two my father was especially concerned about as my grandmother Kate had recently died at the house, and why he told my mother at evacuation time, "Take the girls and I'll follow later". So many would have said the same to their wives, but everything had to be decided so quickly, hence many men were left on their own.

History of the World

Bullet in Spine makes Radio History

My uncle Reg was serving with the Royal Light Infantry and was injured at Cambrai in France in 1917. The German raid at the harbour must have been an awful reminder of this time when he was severely wounded and a bullet was lodged near his spine. Since that time, he had been an invalid and had spent long periods in UK hospitals. Due to the bullet being so close to his spine, an operation was impossible all those years ago, but on January 30th 1936, after 19 years, surgeons at the Queen Mary Hospital in London with new knowledge and skill, removed the bullet. This he kept as a momento of those painful years.

Young Uncle Reg as a soldier and at Roehampton

He then had to stay and recuperate in hospital for another 14 weeks. I can't say how many months or years he spent in different hospitals during those 19 years of waiting, but I remember him well being a cheerful and lovely uncle, and before the occupation my mother visited him at Roehampton Hospital in the UK. Uncle Reg and other seriously injured men on the wards, kept themselves busy by making belts and jewellery out of cellophane to pass the time away.

During October 2010, items were being asked for a collection of interesting items for 'A History of the World' programme on the BBC. I decided to take Uncle Reg's bullet and it was photographed at the Candie Museum. I was surprised to hear from a Mr Tom Aubin, a presenter from Radio 4, who wanted to include the bullet in his programme and spoke of the time of 1917 in France when Reginald Collins received his injuries and how he was severely handicapped through it. Sadly, Uncle Reg died on November 30th 1941, aged 48 years, at the hospital in Guernsey.

Uncle Bill at the harbour

Another uncle and son of Gran and Grandpa (Pop) was William ('Bill') Collins, who was also seriously injured in the First World War, and lost his entire arm. Having a shoe shop situated in Pollet Street, he too must have felt the harbour raid was an awful reminder of his injuries and pain. He worked and ran his large premises selling shoes for many years (known as W.J. Collins), but gradually, with the occupation and less stock coming from France, he like all other shops either had to close or just stay open for one day or two during the week, and was a 'barter and exchange' shop.

I wish I had asked more about my father's life when he was a young man, as I am sure it would have been very interesting – he was quite a character and a lovely man, hardworking and sporty, being a football referee and a water polo player before the war and a States diver, finding items around the coast, but mostly around the harbour.

I have his discharge papers from the army after being thrown out on 29 March 1920. Dad was born on June 7th 1903 but stated his birth date was 1902, and was in the army for just one year and 56 days! He was discharged after the mis-statement of age was discovered, but I must add his character and conduct during his time and his 'military career' was stated to have been good for the whole time!

Les Côtils (The Blue Mountains) and Castle Carey

In 1940 our family had settled well into Rose Villa, Les Canichers. I have always felt if we had not moved to number 30 (as it was also known) I probably would not have had an interesting story to tell. Everything was centred around our busy road and we were living very central for the 'stores', and we were beneath the Côtils, and near the Esplanade, harbour and town with lovely sea views of the islands and harbour.

'Les Côtils' building is now a Christian retreat and conference centre and also caters very well for holiday guests. Before the war, it was run as a school for kindergarten age children, run by French, American and French Canadian

View looking over St Peter Port Harbour from a 60cm German searchlight position at Les Cotils. Our house is situated below, and the back of the Royal Hotel is centre photo. *(CIOS)*

teaching nuns, and the scholars had a bi-lingual education. Besides the school and convent, the nuns ran a farm with a large herd of cows supplying milk and butter. In their large grounds, they also had pigs, rabbits and hens. At evacuation time, at least 12 pupils evacuated to Cheshire and the remaining children joined another boarding school at 'La Chaumière' in Guernsey. With such a large building and rooms, the nuns decided to run a 'care home' for the elderly, but in 1941 the Guernsey authorities needed extra beds, wanting an annexe to the Town Hospital for the elderly.

With the hospital only running for a year and just being settled, one day's notice was then given as the Germans wanted the building for themselves. The order had been given and had to be obeyed but one can appreciate the upset and upheaval having to move out and settle 68 elderly patients within 24 hours. Especially with the shortage of vehicles suitable for the removal of these patients – it was a mammoth job. The beds were heavy oak, held together by long bolts, easily taken apart but very difficult to put back together as the bolts did not fit, and nails had to be used.

The Germans considered the building and grounds were in a vantage position. Looking out from the top of the Blue Mountains (Les Côtils) was the ideal vantage point for four 10.5 cm coastal artillery guns, which was an important part of the Harbour Blocking Battery. Big Berthas (we called them) and did we know it when they fired! Some 500 and 850lb bombs were used. These enormous guns above our home resulted in the family having to leave the house very early at times being 5am or 6am and windows and doors had to be left open, until we were allowed back at a specific time. 'ACTUNG! ACTUNG!' we'd hear, 'Schnell', which meant we had to clear out quickly! Our house suffered damage, including the ceilings falling down in the attic. Even the elderly patients at the old Town Hospital (now Police Station) had to move out during this time. It was at these times that my father would be annoyed and I can only imagine what my grandfather was thinking and saying under his breath and you will read later, why – the secret he kept!

Situated opposite Les Côtils centre is Castle Carey, a large imposing residence where eventually Germans had an 'Officers Club'. It was two officers from the club who approached my sister and I in the street one day, and asked if we were hungry. As we were, we naturally answered quickly "Ja, danke", then one of them told us to go home and collect containers and

The 60cm German searchlight being returned to the storage shelter at Les Cotils. (CIOS)

explained to go through the bottom back door and walk up the long gardens of Castle Carey to the kitchens and see the chefs. This was normally not allowed in this area because of the guns, searchlights and firing practice which was held at times on Cambridge Park, but there was no hesitation. My mother eagerly found the largest jug and saucepan in the kitchen and off we went together while the offer was there. The German chefs in their kitchen seemed pleased to give us the thick, white barley soup and as we walked back down through the 'mad' lanes and down many steps to Rose Villa, we never spilt a drop! I can only think since, that for us allowed to go out of bounds anywhere on our own, any extra food must have been a godsend for my mother.

In 1940, at the beginning of the Occupation, all Islanders felt that within six months, all the Germans would be gone and would be back to normal life again, that was wishful thinking! A notice was given 'hoarding of food was forbidden, all housewives to sign and declare that no more than one month's reserve was to be kept' but with that – many rushed out to buy. This included my mother as food stocks were fairly plentiful and my mother tried to buy in as much as she could – not to be greedy but thought if the war and Occupation lasted for 6 months, at least we'd have 'a little something' in the cupboard. The few tins and packets we had of tea, sugar etc. soon dwindled but Mum tried to keep a tin of meat or fruit for a special occasion. Of course, if the Occupation had only lasted for 6 months we would have fared quite well but as it was a very long six months the 'little something' we had did not last and the many special occasions outweighed our few tins and packets, especially having six hungry males and two growing daughters to bring up and look after! I often wonder now how my mother managed it. I suppose black marketing helped as it wasn't long before our weekly food ration was small and gradually getting smaller.

Mum and Dad had to spend savings at these small barter shops that sprung up in the town either exchanging items or buying items of food if one was lucky at the very beginning for a £1, but with goods getting more scarce as time went by, these items such as a ¼ pound of tea, would cost £7 or £8. £1 was a lot of money in those days but Mum had her money's worth! The precious packet of tea was dried and brewed several times as you can imagine and nothing was wasted. Everything was precious when it came to food.

Queueing for the meat ration in the market, 1940.

1941 – 1942 A Near Miss

Shops were soon emptied as the German troops had time on their hands and plenty of Marks to spend. They mostly bought the expensive goods, such as cameras, shoes, leather goods, clothes, stockings, toiletries and all knitting wool and garments were bought up to send away to their families and loved ones in Germany. Shops in Smith Street in 1941 were all empty and other shops in the town. During 1941, the German troops were arriving by the thousands. A thousand at a time and without warning, accommodation had to be found straight away. The foreign slave workers (TODT Organisation) too were reaching maximum numbers and they needed accommodation until houses and billets could be offered. All hotels were taken over and it was only the Royal Hotel that continued functioning as a hotel. All the elementary schools except for Torteval School were being occupied and taken over. As regards the secondary schools, Elizabeth College and the two intermediate schools were also occupied. Elizabeth College was an emergency hospital; the Boys' Intermediate School became a billet and the Girls' School, a food store.

It was at this time there was widespread talk of Islanders being thrown out of their homes at short notice for the troops to move into and just being allowed personal items to take with them. Some were offered to stay with Germans in the house but the lady would have to wash their clothes. My aunt and grandmother, my father's sister and mother who also lived in St Peter Port were given the choice either to move out or could stay and have the Germans live in their choice of rooms, but my aunt would have to wash their clothing and bedding. Because of my gran's age, my aunt decided

Troops choosing gifts, Press Shop, Smith Street
with courtesy of Simon Hamon.

Troops passing the Royal Hotel (now offices on the Glategny Esplanade) 1940.

to stay and although there was an incident when the officers were really annoyed with my gran and threatened prison(!), they apparently caused no trouble and these Germans kept to themselves. I remember my aunt saying sometimes, mostly officers, would come and go and when they had food occasionally, they would give my aunt a treat for their tea and it was eggs that were given (more in 'Reflections of Guernsey'). With all this talk of Germans taking over houses, my mother must have been aware of this. I remember the time very well in 1941 when I was at home one morning with mum when we heard the heavy boots coming up the path. We were very fortunate to be allowed to stay in our home for the duration as it was only the very quick thinking of my mother that did it. The German officers arrived at the door and wanted to look over the house. We knew why they wanted to look it over. Les Canichers, where we lived, was a very busy street, there always being plenty of activity with German soldiers.

It was also very important to live near the Harbour, also the Royal Hotel and one house eventually later on, just opposite, was a departure centre or Depot for many young soldiers being sent to Russia to fight. All these happenings were around us and Mum and I guessed that our home could well be in line for Officers to live in. So, on this day when we spotted the

Officers coming up the path, Mum just knew what the outcome could be. They started with the top floor with us walking behind them and dreading with every step what the outcome would be, we knew with six bedrooms with harbour and lovely island sea views as well, everything would be 'Prima'. We knew this word well and they kept repeating it to each other! Coming down a flight of stairs and on to the first landing, my mother gave me a nudge and a wink, and started groaning and moaning! She fell on to the floor and as I leaned over and muttered 'What's wrong Mum?' she whispered 'Shh, be quiet - ooh, ahh', the moaning seemed so real. The Germans looked concerned and asked 'Was ist laus?' 'Was ist laus?' I answered and said Mum was sick, with that they must have believed it - they took a look at my face and my mother's and that must have been enough as off they went and we never saw them again. Quick thinking by my mother and what a blessing, as with all the rooms 'prima' our family would probably have had two or three hours to move out with just a few personal belongings. Clothes only – everything else the Germans would have stepped in and lived with for the duration of the Occupation. Many people experienced this and there was always the threat of it happening at any time. This was the first time that soldiers had come to the house but indeed, it was not the last. Another twice which were certainly not friendly visits!

Although, to their credit, another two came - an officer and his batman had been living in my aunt's house nearby at the top of Bosq Lane (as she had evacuated) and they asked my mother if she would like to have photographs they had come across of our family and my aunt? The officer spoke very good English and felt because he was leaving, there would probably be more troops coming to live at the house and they might destroy them. They returned with the photographs and my mother appreciated this and kept them until my aunt returned after the war. Mum and dad felt they probably had a family back home in Germany and they were decent men as a lot of them were. Unfortunately for them, they said they were being sent to Russia within a day or two.

At the Headquarters opposite at a house called 'Olinda', next to 'Grangeclare', the young German soldiers we used to see dreaded the thought of being sent to Russia especially if they had to go in the depths of winter with the weather so bitterly cold. Guernsey must have seemed like a paradise to them. Many a time we saw these young soldiers hiding in our gardens amongst the bushes trying to evade the count, when they were all lined up along the street.

We did know of German soldiers trying to injure themselves to prevent going on active service and on to the Russian Front. They would deliberately fall over our garden walls into the narrow part of the road below and we did hear that two died because of head injuries. We used to see the Officers treating these men roughly and there was always plenty of commotion, but as regards to any receiving fatal injuries, nothing was written about such happenings. Only this past Christmas 2013, I received greetings from an ex-German soldier (whom I had never met) wrote to say "Guernsey saved my life by not sending me to Russia and I could stay in nice Guernsey". This was a complete surprise but he felt like others I am sure, that Guernsey was a good, safe place to be and he had never forgotten it.

At other times to us children it was also comical to see the enemy all dressed up and camouflaged in multi colours with large twigs and branches sticking out from their helmets. It was a usual sight to see them hopping over our garden walls and hiding behind our bushes, playing at manoeuvres.

La Vallette and Alderney:
Clothes gathered from the sea!

Alderney was more or less completely evacuated but it was felt a little later that it was a wrong decision because men were now needed for maintenance and for some agriculture work and to generally watch over the interests of the Island. A heavy crop of potatoes were ready to be dug and many of the houses at that time in early 1941 had been ransacked and general clearing had to be done. Some 20-30 men were sent from Guernsey to work there for a period.

I remember a time when walking near La Vallette Swimming Pools when I vividly remember seeing many people coming away from the childrens' pool with masses of dripping wet clothes, items of small furniture and toys etc. They were placing them on bicycles, hand-carts and prams etc. and seemed very pleased with these dripping items. When I was writing my first book in 1985, I asked my mother if she remembered this happening but she could not remember this at all. This surprised me but I can only presume I must have wandered away from her or from friends but this was very vivid to me. I asked several friends at the time but no-one could recall this happening, so decided not to write about it. It was only recently I was looking at an Occupation diary printed by the Reverend Ord from the Rohais and he explained the unusual sight on June 28 1941 when houses in Alderney were emptied and all the clothes etc were brought down to Guernsey. They were verminous and dirty, hence everything was taken to the Children's pool and was well covered by the high tide. The authorities probably felt that the sea

STRANGE DOINGS AT LA VALETTE

CLOTHES GATHERED FROM THE SEA

Strange things are happening at La Valette. The public pool there has been turned into a bargain basement. People are fishing clothes from the sea!

At least 100 Sarnians were on the spot from 7 o'clock this morning adding to their wardrobe as quickly as they could gather the garments that lay at the bottom of the Pool or were strewn on the beach. A steady stream of people who had already made their "purchases," some pushing them in prams, others with heavy bundles wrapped in sheets or eiderdowns, were making for home with their captures.

This remarkable scene needs some explanation. So an "Evening Press" reporter has ascertained why clothing (male and female) should come from the sea in the manner of a fishing catch.

Originally from Alderney—where they had accumulated a fair proportion of livestock during the long period before clearance—the garments were brought to Guernsey. Someone had the bright idea that the clothes would be separated from their little friends if placed in sea-water for some time. Yesterday afternoon a lorry, laden with habiliments, arrived at the Public Pool at La Valette. The driver proceeded to tip the load into the Pool.

It was high tide at the time. Some of the garments sank. A small quantity disappeared out to sea or for the adjacent Mixed Bathing Pool where it was rescued by the attendant and replaced in the Public Pool.

Word was soon spread: not long after the costumes remaining in the Pool were being fished out by local people who were grasping their opportunities with both hands and any grappling irons available.

Then someone had the bright idea of emptying the Pool. Things were made a great deal easier. Clothes were brought up the beach and spread out to dry. From there the bargain hunters could make a more reasoned selection. Babies were left to cry in their prams while Mother chose the little something-or-other that would be about her size. The choice was wide: Anything from a fur coat to ... well! One person is now the proud possessor of an evening dress waistcoat. He is searching anxiously for the rest of the outfit.

Unfortunately the short immersion has not removed the vermin. Before wearing these things it is hoped that the finder will disinfect the garment. Otherwise there will be some scratching and gnashing of teeth.

If this was meant to be a free distribution of clothing, it is the strangest one we have ever encountered.

This is the account that appeared in the local newspaper 1st July 1941

45

water would cleanse them, and even at this time, soon after the German forces arrived, many islanders might have been short of clothing, and it was the norm for people to have box carts or carrier boxes on bicycles or prams. Although the reading of this article is funny in parts, I think it shows that even in 1941 clothes were in very short supply in the shops. There were still families who stayed with several children living in the Southern part of Town, which I am sure took full advantage of taking free clothing and maybe toys for their children.

The pram that my mother, sister and I used was worth its weight in gold during this time, what would we have done without it? You will read later of the games we played.

Later in 1941 and throughout the Occupation, the Vallette was closed to pedestrians (except those with permits) from the bottom of the Val des Terres (from today's Half Moon café), and of course around to the Fort George and all the South Coast and beyond.

The childrens and ladies pool at La Vallette where the Germans built a shelter with courtesy of Simon Hamon.

Law and Orders: Grandpa fooled the Germans

After the German Forces had landed, I remember the Island tried to resume its normal everyday life as best it could, but each day everyone wondered what was going to happen. On the front page of our newspaper were new Laws and Orders to be obeyed without question. I remember one of the first, 'by Order of the Commandant' was for all fire arms to be handed in, ammunition, guns and powder – to be handed in immediately. It was my old grandfather (what a character), my mother's father, that caused the biggest scare during this time. Before the war his favourite hobby was shooting. He owned a gun and made his own cartridges and shells etc. Joe or Pop Collins, as he was affectionately called, was always to be found at 'The Rabbit Warren' whenever he had a chance. Well, the Germans soon put paid to this of course and he was most upset when seeing all firearms of every description had to be handed in at once. I remember well Grandpa 'blessing' the Germans for calling in his prize gun, the very last thing he wanted to hand over as he cherished it always. Well, Pop did hand in a gun and a small amount of gunpowder. Not knowing differently, Mum and Dad thought that was the whole amount of gunpowder and the only gun he had.

Mum and Dad probably did not think too much about these items, they were gone and that was that. Grandpa inwardly must have chuckled until one evening, about 3 years later, 2 German Gestapo burst into our house.

They made it very clear they wanted to search the house and this they did from top to bottom in every room and also our small back yard. We all waited for the verdict but they found nothing and left the house muttering in German. After they had gone, Pop was outside checking inside a barrel of sawdust to see if his prize gun and powder had been disturbed!! Grandpa had handed in a very old gun but kept his favourite well hidden amongst some rubbish and sawdust! My poor mother nearly had a fit on the spot – no-one knew of it being there and if it had been found we would have been lucky in just being sent to Germany in a camp! The outcome would probably have been far worse! Grandpa really should have known better than to put all the family at such risk. "We could have all been shot" I remember my father saying; but it was too late to let the Germans know about these items now, the punishment would have been the same and Mum and Dad dreaded the consequences. Mum and Dad and all of us had to keep quiet about it but my mother and father must have been really worried, thinking always if ever 'they' came again, would they find it?

'They' did come again, and again it must have been our lucky day. It was soon afterwards my grandmother, on Dad's side of the family, and other relations had been invited to join us for a little supper. My mother had recently left hospital after having an operation so it was really a get together and a little celebration.

Mum said a friend, Charlie Smith, had somehow 'acquired' a cow from a farmer and he had walked with this cow from the country through the night to Jory's coal yard in St Julian's Avenue near our home where it was killed by a local butcher and cut into joints for selling! These joints were hidden in an old chest of drawers and discreetly sold on the black market as a price you can just imagine! It was to be a treat for the family so Mum and Dad did not mind the expense for this time. We had just finished enjoying the meal, luckily the plates were clean and I can remember us all sitting around the table in our large room, when we heard the sound of boots coming up the path. Germans did not knock on either of our two entrance doors, not at these times. It was their custom just to burst in to living rooms and try to catch people unaware of their presence. Again, the Gestapo were to search from top to bottom and the yard, but again, muttered and spoke amongst themselves and then walked out. What relief for my mother and father! Afterwards, I always remember, Mum and Dad thinking that perhaps someone had sent an anonymous letter about us having a black market joint of beef! No-one wanted to believe fellow islanders would so such things, but unfortunately, it did happen. Some Islanders did this for whatever reason, but the Post Office sorters did destroy many when they had an idea of what

When the occupation started all traffic was immediately moved to drive on the right hand side of the road. The pictures above show German direction signs. The bottom picture was taken at 'Choisy' at the Queens Road/Les Gravees junction.

More Hidden Treasures: Wireless sets

The Germans issued an order in September 1940 demanding that all wireless (radio) sets were to be handed in, and they were returned in December 1940. The order was re-issued in June 1942 for duration of the Occupation.

My father had a friend, Mr Bill Robilliard, an undertaker from St Peter Port, who offered to hide our wireless set in a coffin! He did so, and had no problems with subsequent searches. The set was returned after the Liberation in good order. So many wireless sets have come to light since the end of the war, having been found in many unusual hiding places. Dad ran a small building firm, and earned great respect from his customers (as it was proved after he died). He worked very hard throughout his life, but especially during the Occupation as the Germans called in his old lorry very early on, and throughout he only had hand push-along trucks to get around, which was not easy with the many hills on Guernsey.

Dad also worked for a Mr Branch, who lived in a large, lovely home in Les Gravées. He asked my father as soon as the Germans arrived, whether Dad would bury all his precious silver in the garden. He was worried that the Germans would want his house and would also take all his prized possessions. Dad did the necessary, and Mr Branch was correct, the Germans very soon moved into his home, but never knew that they were constantly walking over all the wonderful silver, which they would certainly have taken and had sent back to Germany. Dad dug up the silver, which was all in perfect condition, after the Liberation and Mr Branch was thrilled. If I remember correctly, he gave my father a very large silver cup.

One day, Dad acquired a permit to do a little job in Herm. So off he went and whilst he had to stay all day, he realised it was an ormering tide (a local shellfish delicacy). The beaches and seas around Herm had not been fished for quite a while – "Verboten" again – so Dad took a chance and looked for these ormers which at very low tide, can be found underneath and between rocks.

Hard work, but he came home with a very good feed for us (and the family), all hidden amongst his gear on the small boat. Herm was well worth a visit.

So many items and even cars were hidden in barns etc. Lucky for the owners, few were found out and we as a family were very fortunate after two searches, when our 'treasures' were not found.

Others with quick thinking were lucky too. After wireless sets were called in (from June 1942 until the end of the war), many islanders decided to keep them and hope for the best that the Germans would not find out about them. But of course they took serious risks. There were some strange hiding places and wives would help out too if they knew or saw Germans around. They would rush to the bedroom and lay in the bed with the wireless set under the covers or place the set on their tummy. The Germans would think they were pregnant or not well, so one would get away with doing this.

A farmer was particularly upset as his wife, without knowing, had lit a fire in their sitting room. The farmer had hidden their wireless in this room, which generally was not used, but had not told his wife about what he had done. Hence the poor farmer was most upset when a friend called and was looking forward to bringing down the wireless from the chimney. All that came down was a well and truly melted mess and the set had gone up in smoke. You can imagine he was quite upset!

One had to be quick too, for example when one mother saw the Germans coming to the house, her immediate thought was, 'get the radio', which she did and grabbed it quickly, placing it in her baby's pram. With the set and the baby nicely covered with blankets, she walked past her husband who had answered the door to the Germans. Whilst they were talking, the Germans smiled and admired the baby and off they went. The mother and baby only returned when she knew the Germans had gone and the coast was clear.

Easily done and it worked.

The stories of the occupation we laugh at now are of hiding radios, animals etc. but I think this is the funniest story. The Gestapo arrived at a house and the wife answered the door. They made it clear that an anonymous letter had been sent to them saying a wireless was hidden in the house and wanted to search it. The wife took them all through the house but left the bedroom until the last. When they entered and opened the door, the husband was sitting on a commode and groaning loudly. The Germans understood a little English, and the wife explained that her husband suffered terribly from piles! He must have acted well as the Germans believed her although her husband had never had piles in his life! The only discomfort he was going through at the time was sitting with his pants down over the radio! Another successful episode against the 'clever' Gestapo and many similar stories have been told since the war ended.

German Soldiers marching past Town Church, St Peter Port.

Vauvert School and Log Book

The Education Committee must have had many problems at the beginning because so many teachers had evacuated to the UK, but we soon knew that Vauvert School would be my sister's and my school. This was not a Catholic school and no nuns would be teaching, so it was strange at first and different to 'The Notre Dame du Rosaire School' where at assembly we always said the Lord's Prayer in French, and we had many lessons in French. The nuns – Sisters Cecile, Margaret & Françoise, were strict but very good teachers. Mr J Hayes was made the headmaster of Vauvert, and four lady teachers (I remember being Miss Moon, Miss Louvet, Miss Messurvy and Mrs Trory) were very understanding. Even at the first Christmas time in 1940, before we broke up for the holidays, the teachers and the Education Committee had arranged some fun and party games, a sing-a-long and a little present for each of us to go home with.

I expect my mother's fear of leaving the house and of the Germans, installed a little fear in us, but many Germans were soon seen in our road and although we did not like the look of their guns, daggers, big noisy jackboots and helmets, they did not look too vicious, only big and very serious looking. Dad walked us to school at the very beginning but seeing it was only a 10 – 15 minute walk through the town, my sister and I would go together and sometimes meet friends to walk with up St Julian's Avenue as the 'Cressard' family who also lived nearby had also stayed and who attended Vauvert School. Rose was my friend and Joyce and I often went to play in their garden, with her sisters. We soon made friends with many girls and boys at the School.

In 1940, Vauvert School was a large modern building housing several hundred children but with only a few left after the evacuation.

The headmaster, Mr John Hayes, was well liked at the school and eventually had to teach German which was made compulsory in January 1942. (He had previously been imprisoned for a short time, after being caught with a wireless set). Before the beginning of 1942, sentences in German and English were printed daily in the local newspaper for everyone to learn the language.

Mr Hayes decided in December 1940 to produce a small magazine of articles by the scholars, which expressed a hope for better times. In the following three pages of the official Vauvert log book, you might be interested to see especially what Betty and Graham had produced. They were probably aged 12 and 13 at the time and I remember them very well.

Vauvert School Logbook as Produced for Records

Vauvert School for example housed children in three departments, relinquished the Infants department very quickly as a civilian flour store and for almost 4 years until the Germans took the whole building over themselves, the school suffered from vermin, an all pervading dust, and a continuous stream of motor traffic through the dangerous girls and infants playground. By the mercy of providence, no child met with an accident. When radio sets had to be given up in November 1940, island officials took the upper storey of the school as a repository for innumerable sets and sent a civilian staff to take care of them. These radio set mechanics eventually came to operate a repair depot for radios in German hands, and for some years a constant stream of motor and horse-drawn traffic crossed and re-crossed the boys yard with damaged and repaired wireless sets. Other schools were similarly used for civilian purposes, but Vauvert, being the largest building had to contribute most. The enemy took over the premises of school after school, until at the end of the year, only 3 publicly owned schools were with the council – Vauvert, Torteval and Sarel schools.

Radio sets were stored but also flour was upstairs, and it was tempting for the boys to take flour from time to time when being excused. We guessed this was happening. We often saw them with bags or bulging pockets. For myself and friends during playtime, we would go through a hole in the

The

Vauvert

CHRISTMAS School. 1940

MAGAZINE.

- Nº1 -

EDITORIAL

If a School, like a Church, consists of the persons
who are members, rather than of the building and its
furnishings, it will not be true to call this the Magazine
of Vauvert School.

We who now occupy these seats of learning are the
non-evacuated residue from a round dozen schools.
Not a few of us are scholastic orphans. Our one-time
class-rooms no longer re-echo with the healthy sounds of
jubilant youth, for there, sacks of flour and mute radios
hold their silent sway.
Others of us are in our own old rooms and find the unwonted
presence of strangers a little confusing.

But the strangeness of the first few weeks is now
wearing off. We are beginning to call our new acquaintances
'friends'. Our days have taken on the ordered sequence we
knew in the past and the wheels of study are turning once
more. We are beginning to look on Vauvert School, as it is
to-day, as 'Our School'.

We ask you, Reader, to look upon this effort
kindly. It is our first and we could hope it will be
our last. It will help to knit us more together into what
can truly be called a School and in days to come it may
prove a tangible link with our life to-day which may then
appear even stranger than it does now.

A LETTER TO FATHER CHRISTMAS

Vauvert School,

10th Dec 1940.

Dear Father Christmas,

It is perhaps too much to expect you to visit us this year. The sky over Guernsey is rather dangerous but if you could arrange to come in a Junkers 52 I suppose you would get here in safety. I hoping you will come: we have just had the chimney swept specially for you so that your white fur will not get dirty, and my pillow-case will be in its usual place at the foot of the bed so that you will be able to leave what you have brought without having to fumble much in the blackout.

Could you bring me some chocolate ?, I have not had any for three months. I would adore a good hunk of Dutch cheese also, and about two dozen eggs would be lovely, if you could get them across without breaking them. Even one egg would be very acceptable. Christmas dinner will not be its usual self without a leg of pork so if you could slip one into my pillow-case I would be very thankful.
I know all this is rather a lot to ask you but you usually manage to provide our requirements.
Oh,-and dont forget the fruit,-oranges,dates and nuts. Lemons are not so important.

I wouldn't mind a few toys but the townspeople are kindly taking on your job this year as regards toys and if you are only going to bring playthings,perhaps you had better not risk the trip. Anyway,I hope you have a safe journey,if you do decide to make the attempt,and that you will not find it necessary to camouflage your reindeer,

Yours,
Betty Boswell.

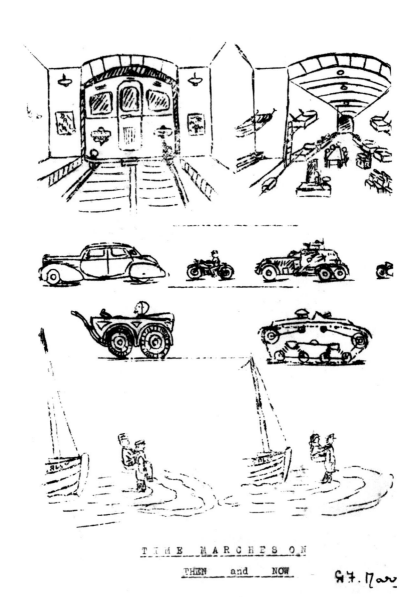

TIME MARCHES ON

THEN and NOW

wooden fence and go scrumping in the next door garden for apples when in season. The house was empty and the owner had probably evacuated. We were never missed at playtime, but perhaps the teachers turned a blind eye to what we were up to!

What was not so pleasant was seeing the slave workers, as before going into school in the morning, they being ill and neglected, were queuing to be seen at a large house next to the school. It was a hospital for the slave workers. Before I had read the account of these poor and underfed men, a school friend had told me of himself and boys could see quite clearly by looking over the wall of the playground, the burning of clothes and the bodies being carried away in makeshift coffins. In the town area and in Vauvert road, and in nearby George Street, there were several houses that housed many of these workers. In 1941/1942, they were arriving from Europe and they were described as being in "verminous condition". 30 deaths were recorded in 1943 and venereal disease occurred in 1942. Scabies and impetigo were widespread but the nurse would regularly check our health. Typhus was confirmed amongst the workers, but when found with the sickness they

St Sampson's School – occupied

were made to stay in billets under guard. At one time there were workers from 36 different countries on the island, and in May 1943, 5100 were on the island. There were several cases of typhoid occurred (also three islanders). Not surprising when we all remember the condition in which they were living, and in many over-crowded country districts. The death rate rose amongst the locals and days were lost through sickness.

The islanders felt so sorry for these men but it was a serious offence if caught helping one. The house, Rose-Adèle across the street where we moved into in 1969 had foreign workers living there for a time, and I remember seeing them very poorly dressed going off to work each morning and very hungry queuing for soup nearby at the bottom of Bosq Lane in the evening. It was so difficult to try and help them. Dad was tempted when seeing them together in our street and without the guard seeing him, sometimes he would manage to give a cigarette to one. I remember seeing a French foreign worker at home coming from time to time whilst they lived at Rose-Adèle, and although seeing him sitting at our table I don't remember seeing him ever eat a meal. Knowing my mother so well, he would probably have been given a little something to eat later at Rose-Adèle.

It was while talking to Malcolm Woodland who attended Hautes Capelles School, he told me of workers living in huts at L'Islet, who had no toilets, just trenches in the field. The labourers had to empty the trenches and load the sewage into a 1,000 gallon greenhouse water tank which had been mounted on a horse-drawn cart, to be taken to the Houmet on the North West coast and dispersed at sea. You can imagine the awfulness of seeing this happening which Malcolm and his friends did.

At Vauvert School, there were notices on the gate and high wire screens, trying to stop the fouling of the school lavatories and the playgrounds, but it continued and some children suffered various infections and venereal disease. Other cases occurred in other island schools. Pleased to say my sister and I had no serious illnesses throughout, and that went for the almost 1000 children who stayed, but again mothers were severely worried seeing these notices, and there was no way of us attending another St Peter Port school. Many of the country children were being moved several times to have lessons, at hotels, churches, schoolrooms or large houses, as the military wanted the schools for storage etc. The children from Vauvert School were moved to St Josephs School for the last year of Occupation, as the Germans took over the whole school for themselves.

To sum up, these words were written after the Occupation in the school logbook.

At Vauvert School, where a building at the school gate was in use as a hospital for foreign workers, the children used to watch the dead being carried out through the school yard, and the infected clothing was incinerated. Protests from the school to the medical of health met with the reply that the children were in no danger. Vauvert School suffered greatly from the close proximity of this; O-T Revier (hospital) as for each morning a group of sick labourers are collected at the school gate waiting for the Revier to open; and notices on the gate and high wire screens failed to prevent the repeated and abominable fouling of the school lavatories and playgrounds.

Some children were unfortunate enough to suffer more than threats of various infections and several instances are known at school of children contracting venereal disease. At Vauvert School a six year old girl was absent for more than 6 months for this reason, and 4 children from the same school were incarcerated with their mother and elder sister in a special VD hospital for a matter of several weeks. There were other cases in other schools.

At one time there were workers in the island from 36 different countries and they would arrive in verminous condition. Several cases of typhoid occurred, including three islanders, which was not surprising with the foreign workers and with gross over-crowding, and large numbers living together without sanitary arrangements. Skin diseases, scabies and impetigo and vermin were quite a concern and widespread through a great shortage of soap.

While it is true that the burden of life weighed most heavily on older people, particularly on those who were living in the town, and were limited to the official rations, it is also true that the war years brought hardships enough to the children. Records of weight showed that a number of children were receiving insufficient food for adequate growth, but in most cases health was maintained, but growth was unsatisfactory.

Life inside school must be made happy and secure – above all happy, even if that might mean some sacrifice of scholastic attainment. Many children were compelled to shoulder responsibilities and play their part in maintaining the home as children have not needed to for many generations past. There was fuel to be got in one way or another. There was everlasting queuing for vegetables, for fish, for the daily hot meal cooked at the bake house. Numerous families found it necessary to scour the country parishes in search of extra vegetables. It is not surprising that many of the normal joys of childhood were unknown to Occupation children.

Peter Girard's wrote in his "Guernsey" book, "On the whole, children were well treated and only once he saw a child assaulted by a German on the last day of the Occupation. He had just told the children that the war was over and they were rushing down Vauvert cheering and shouting with joy, when without warning a passing German hit a child right across the face. The child was not really hurt so no further action was taken."

Mr Girard had also written in his book, children remained free from the usual childrens' illnesses. Influenza was rather serious in one period and 'occupation dysentery' was a constant worry, especially when typhus broke out amongst the foreign slave workers. The shortage of good soap and nutrition led to skin complaints which only cleared up after liberation.

Queuing for vegetables at The French Halls in the Town Market.

Hautes Capelles School, St Sampson

The Daily Log Book stated:

1940 August 26th – Air raid practice

August 27th – German officer asked for room upstairs and key for instruction of soldiers.

August 28-30th – Daily air raid practice

September 3rd – German soldiers stationed in district drilled in our school yard before morning school. (I was also told this by a friend, Malcolm Woodland who began school there at age 5-6 and found so many soldiers in the playground a bit un-nerving, he being so young.)

Fire drills and air raid practices continue often. Better news on October 21st 1940. A half pint of whole milk was delivered for the first time – free of charge for every child at the school.

There was a period when the school closed when unexploded bombs were found close by, and the children from Hautes Capelles were moved to different premises many times during the five years. During the winter of 1941, bitterly cold weather kept children at home because most had heavy colds and they were without good shoes. Many children did not attend schools on Tuesday or Thursday mornings because they would have had no bread for breakfast until the bread was collected from the shops. Rationed bread was only issued on Tuesday, Thursday and Saturdays.

When school re-opened on January 9th 1941, a soup kitchen had opened at the Hautes Capelles Methodist Church Sunday School which must have been a blessing for many parents to know over 120 of their children from the school had a good dinner, and the dinners were continued for the school every Tuesday and Thursday while supplies were available (charge was 1 penny, about half a pence in today's money).

Come 1942 and by this time some children did not have any shoes or warm clothing at all, and had been ill for many months. Three boys from one family had been at home for 9 weeks with no fit clothing or shoes and when eventually some wooden soled shoes came from France, they were expensive at over £1.50 (weekly wages were average £2-£3) and did not last long. I remember having wooden soled shoes and we had to have 20 minutes of frequent exercising because of having 'flat' feet.

A Very Great Treat: A third gift of biscuits eaten daily at school was a gift from 'Le Secours National de France'. Apparently they had sent biscuits 7 times between 1942 and 1944 to this particular school. (I had previously remarked on the joy of having a surprise biscuit with our school milk. I will always remember that, and the pleasure of Mr Mauger, our care-taker giving it to us.)

A different account of biscuits was written by a friend of mine, entitled:

Private Schools Education during Occupation Years 1940-1945

We had an issue of biscuits for school children but they were uneatable however hungry you were, and we were! They had to be broken up with a heavy tool of some sort. One of the boys said they were ship's biscuits and meant to last a voyage of years. Obviously we couldn't eat them at the school break time, so we could take them home. One wet day with no break outside, we had to stay in the schoolroom, so a game was devised by throwing the biscuits against the wall and whoever was the strongest would break the biscuit first. Great fun, but with so much noise falling on to the floor boards, Miss M called out the names for caning, and shouting 'a thousand lines' in her temper. Lines were reduced with second thoughts because of the shortage of paper – therefore 200 lines were written.

At the small school where Fay was taught during the five years, she wrote of the strict discipline of the school and boys and girls were taught there from the age of four to twelve years. Pencils were only sharpened by Miss M the teacher, and being scarce there were no more to be had, only what the education department would allow for the school. When the pencil showed just above the thumb and forefinger, one could have a new one. The ink from

France was awful and Miss M kept her supply in a container and each week refilled their glass inkwells, but the ink lay as black as mud. When stirred gently it was useable, but the boys would dip their nib too far and would write with black hands, hence this wasted paper that was in short supply so the cane was used. After bending over the boy would get 'three of the best'! It was not really a cane but it was a two foot long thick piece of wood, which the teacher held with her two hands whilst the boy bent over in front of her. (I am sure the boys would have had more than a red face when they went back to their seats). Girls would have at least a hundred lines to write for punishment for whatever reason. Fay had spoken to some of the former pupils when they were in their 'seventies', and not one of them like Fay regretted the discipline they had because they knew it was deserved.

Amongst Fay's many memories that she gave to me, she wrote of when in 1943 English born men and families were to be deported to German internment camps. Miss M told the children they would meet 7 year old Robin for the last time the next morning as he was to also leave. Fay never thought she would see him again as he was a pale skinned boy with lovely curly fair hair and she thought he would be unable to survive in harsh conditions in a camp and in a cold enemy country. However, she was pleased and surprised when Robin gladly did come back. An older boy Fay played with died of Meningitis in the camp and sadly his parents had to leave their only son buried in the enemy country. Kay writes: *as children it is easier to accept such times, but later as adults you remember and will never forget*.

It was early in 1945, Miss M told the children of a new boy almost 4 years old coming as a pupil to the school. His mother was a local lady and his father a German soldier. The children were warned that if they spoke of the German father they would be severely punished. The boy joined two other four year olds, and sat with them for lessons.

In Fay's own words, she wrote of happier times and summed up her thoughts: *Liberation day came at last and in June our King and Queen came to Candie Gardens where all the school assembled. King George VI and Queen Elizabeth were quite small people, but our own Bailiff was even smaller as he climbed the stairs to the stage. For us, these were the important people of course, not the large impressive German officers we had been used to seeing, strutting about.*

Behind us now were the five years of occupation, trying to write 'properly' during the winter with our fingers swollen with chilblains, in spite of excellent ointment issued by the Germans and our fingers bandaged. Remembering the times spent in the cellar under the school during an air raid, damp and dark down there it was!

So we all moved on in September to the big schools some of us had once attended. Difficult times for us teenagers, as so many of the pupils had been learning the usual curriculum for the Oxford School Certificate and although we were proved by testing to have had just as 'good' an education, in fact better in some instances, we only had three years in which to study for the five year S.C. certificate. Initially we all suffered from the previous lack of nourishment; gym, swimming, games were unknown to us, and lack of muscle tone was obvious in the first year. I never ceased to appreciate the little school where we were taught the pleasure of the learning for its own sake by the lady who had been taught by a governess. She was fluent in French, German, Latin and Greek, and could teach algebra and geometry had we been 'up to it'. She taught everything possible to us hungry and often very cold pupils as there was no heating available the last winter at home or at school. It was her triumph and our everlasting benefit. (What lovely words thinking of Miss M, the teacher.)

Even though there were few pupils at the private school, they would have an annual inspection by a lovely lady they came to know well, who was also known by Fay's parents. Her mother was very annoyed, though knowing the children also had visits by the German officer inspector. However, her father helped the situation by explaining that the occupying authorities' forces had to ensure that the children were being educated to a good standard and children of ten years had to learn good German from the booklet they provided. Miss M told the children that each in turn would go to the officer with samples of their work for him to examine. Firstly, he shook hands with Miss M and bowed to her. When he finished examining Fay's work, he spoke in perfect English that her work was 'good'. Fay was most impressed when he also bowed over her hands and clicked his heels in his high black boots. She told her Dad about it when she got home, and he said as I was a 'senior' at ten years old, this was a gentleman's custom for acknowledging a lady! (Hopefully that might have helped to please her mother!)

A young Malcolm Woodland on the right of the photo with a flag and I am side faced to the left of the King's shoulder, at Candie Gardens. June 7th 1945. The teacher from my school, Miss M Moon on right taking a photograph.

Malcolm Woodland, Stan and Leslie Bichard

Although this visit of an officer to Fay did not seem to worry her, one can imagine how a meeting such as this could affect anyone shy and timid. Malcolm, who passed the exam from Hautes Capelles School to the Intermediate School in 1944 and at 10 years old, had started to learn German, and had heard of the dreaded German teacher Mrs Tate at our school. He dreaded knowing a German officer would enter the class from time to time and could ask him questions. These would have to be answered correctly to please the officer! When I mentioned these times in my talks to groups and Malcolm is present, I always sense that the worry was very real and he will never forget how he felt at these times, and yes, he admits he was very scared.

The Germans loved marching and singing for hours it seemed, and a different Malcolm joined other young boys and marched behind the singing Germans. They would go home and make 'guns' and other weapons, and sing as well, but would make up their own wording!! We shall guess to what the words were! The Germans would sing constantly this song – you would hear their marching and with three abreast with an NCO marching at their side – then suddenly a large loud shout like a crack of a whip, then counting 1 2 3, then they would all sing loudly, which sounded like 'I E I O aya'. The chorus of the favourite marching song and one of which we most tired of hearing follows:

Heili heilo

Heili heilo

Heili heila

Heila ha ha ha ha!

Heili heilo – and repeat again, and again, and again.

Behind these troops would be the boys and some would put their cap on back to front and add twigs and leaves over their faces as if they were on manoeuvres.

Malcolm can also claim to have had a ride with a high ranking officer in a big posh car and watching the speedometer raise to 60 miles an hour. He and his young friend directed the German to where he wanted and they were thanked in perfect English. He was also asked for the direction of 'The Bridge' by a German sitting on one of their large horses. The German was puzzled where all the water was, and the boats? He coaxed Malcolm to have a ride on his tame horse, and before he could refuse, the German picked Malcolm up and on his own, Malcolm took the reins and trotted off down the street and came back. He was a well-trained horse, but Malcolm laughing said he felt grateful to get down from this big horse, and then showed the German how to find the Bridge and the water. Talking of these horses they were certainly very large and beautiful horses, and the Germans brought over 1000, but there were only about 600 left at the end of the Occupation. Probably many were eaten by the hungry troops, as they did cats and dogs during the last year. The horses that were left, were auctioned off to islanders after the Occupation.

Stan Bichard is a well-known Guernsey character and musician on the island (my age), and he also did the same thing with his young friends, but got up to more serious antics than marching. Near the family's home at Les Grifon (behind St George estate) there was a German NAAFI of three huts with goodies for the troops. Keeping out of sight, when the coast was clear they would get to the telephone and cause 'an emergency'! The Germans straight away would rush out to the view-finder and searchlight to know what was happening. Then the 4 boys would get into action themselves and collect the treats at the NAAFI. Unfortunately, after a few successes, they were caught.

They also cut telephone wires as they were laid along in trenches, so the boys (aged about 8 or 9 at this time) got away with doing this too for a while, but Stan said 'we all had many clips around the ears from the troops when caught'.

Grown up men had more than this when caught doing the same thing. Other groups of men would have to patrol all night around the airport and St Martins area in all weathers and the area of the Castel. If Germans found wires cut or if any one got caught, the penalty could have been death.

Recently, hearing Stan talking of his memoirs and what he and his friends got up to, mentioned a particular time when he 'connected' with a high ranking German officer which could have been serious. The young group of boys including his brother Les, were behind a hedge having a game of throwing turf at bicycles as they passed. Then one boy shouted "there's a car coming!" and with that, Stan's handful went straight through an open window of the car into the face of the German officer! Stan and the others made a quick getaway and stayed hidden for a couple of hours in the bushes until they felt the coast was clear. Unfortunately, PC Le Cocq was passing on his bicycle at the time, and had to report the incident. For punishment, each boy had to write and apologise to the FeldKommandantur. This punishment could have been worse, but bad enough at the time for the boys to write to this important man. No reply was given!

In my class at the Intermediate School was Les (Stan's brother) who really upset Mrs Tate (the German teacher) and she was furious! At one lesson, she was telling the class how London was heavily bombed and seemed proud of the fact. With that, Les answered (remembering him as quite a lad!) said, "Well, Berlin was flattened too last night!". With that, she went for Les in really a bad temper, hitting out at him so much that some boys had to restrain her. Les certainly had more than a clip around the ear, but more could have been the consequence of this as next day the Germans turned up at the house and wanted to search, thinking that a radio or crystal set was hidden. They had no radio, but Stan said the Germans who were living next door had one, and the 'bat-man' (high ranking officers always had a 'bat-man') would invite the boys' father to listen to the BBC news when he was at the house alone, and they would listen together.

Stan feels that the majority of troops here were alright if you behaved yourself (I feel the same and others too), as he had also been given the boot, like I had, but he had also been given a few sweets when asking them for "bonbons"! Even when asking "Cig for Papa?" he wasn't disappointed, as he was usually given a couple to take home for his dad.

The Germans were mainly kind to (especially young) children. Many Germans had families and children back in Germany. John, an old school friend, told me he was offered a loaf from a German which he was eager to take – but then the Germans asked "have you sisters?" Yes said John, and what age the Germans asked. John replied, "16 and 17". Then the German said "Can I meet one of them and then perhaps go out with her?" John had to laugh and say "No, she's in England, she evacuated". Lucky for John, he saw the funny side of cheeky John and gave him the bread. These are the times we older ones can laugh about, but it wasn't so funny at the time.

A German band playing outside the Town Market.

Food 1941-1942

Food was always on our minds, especially for my mother having to feed my father, grandfather, three uncles whose wives had evacuated, a 17 year old cousin Ted, my sister, myself and of course herself. Every morning at about 7.30am, before the markets opened, Mum would queue for an hour or two, hoping seasonal vegetables would come in from the farms. After the Germans had taken their quota, mum would hopefully buy enough for a vegetable soup in the evening. Marjorie Bird wrote in her book, "we had to queue for even the smallest amount. A parsnip maybe and a swede would always be cut in half and sold to two people." She also wrote "we grated raw potatoes and fried the peel, the potato peel was far more appetising than eating potatoes with their skin on."

Even before the real shortage in 1944-1945, the year 1942 was, I'm sure, a real worry for my parents, and I feel that they went without food for us, like other parents during this time.

Early in 1942, the very cold weather in winter brought a real concern as there were no potatoes for many weeks at times on ration, no sugar, no meat and no cheese. It was estimated that the grown-ups at most were having 1072 calories a day.

All food was severely rationed during the spring, the Guernsey authorities wanted to contact the Red Cross requesting food, but Jersey said it might interfere and stop food coming in from France and instead of getting some regular food, it might be that they would stop altogether, leaving all shipments to the Red Cross. This probably would have been the case.

Thankfully, Mr Raymond Falla (the States purchasing agent) worked tirelessly and did make many visits to France and soon after the German forces arrived in 1940, he spent two months there buying and securing food for the Islands. This continued throughout until June 1944 when trips had to stop because of the D Day Landing.

Barley came from France at times and this was mixed for a substitute coffee – this would have been grated with roasted acorns or grated parsnips. I remember the parsnip coffee was quite nice (if sugar was available). Joyce and I would collect many acorns and take them to the shops who were paying 3d a pound as they were needed for drinks. Sugar beet, wheat, beans and lupin seeds which were roasted and ground were also tried and used. Recipes were given such as sweetcorn pudding, carrageen relish, potato sandwich, parsnip pudding, tomato pie, limpet omelette etc. Every commodity was naturally on ration and they could change week by week. Flour, sugar, butter, cooking fat, bread and even milk.

We children had to also play our part by queuing and helping to keep the family with food and commodities. I remember mum and I walking a long way with our pram twice a week to St Martin's Dairy and queuing for buttermilk when it was available, taking cans with us. We walked back home for Mum to make some kind of sweet for a change. We would also walk to St Andréws and L'Ancresse on other days hoping for vegetables. When Carrageen moss was allowed to be collected from the beaches, it was then dried and powdered and available to buy from the chemists. If one could add flavouring it would form a jelly, and Mum would make a sweet for us.

Buying on the Black Market was big business. Rations were so low if locally grown food was available, pricing was high, such as butter £1, and eggs etc. (remembering a man's average weekly wage was £2-3). Most of the locals knew where Black Market goods could be had if one had money to spare, but one lady walked from the country to town as she heard food was plentiful at the 'Black Market'. She surely must have had quite a shock when she saw the prices!

Not only food, but tobacco and cigarettes were also strictly rationed. There were sale or exchange notices in the Press and someone advertised from 38 Victoria Road with quite a selection: "Baby's teat for rising powder, Lovely pre-war pink wool dressing jackets, Gents' real hair brushes (leather case), Grate guard, Soft hand brushes, Baby's shoes size 1, 50 gramophone needles, Yeast vite, Kaolin poultice, Cream curtains, Life size baby doll, Exchange for local cigs or good local tobacco, or what permissible". So many items offered for food and/or cigarettes.

At Christmas time after the war
– Grandpa enjoying his pipe

My pop tried to smoke everything and anything, including rose petals in his pipe. He stank the place out with all the horrible smells! With only having 20 cigarettes or 1 ounce of tobacco a week, you can imagine how the men especially, would try anything at this time. Cigarettes were made from locally grown tobacco and packets of twenty were selling for 35 marks, almost £4 and tasted awful and smelt like a bonfire when being smoked. Tobacco mixed with vine leaves and even lettuce, and again bramble leaves were dried. I can see my old grandfather now, smoking his pipe and what was in it was anyone's guess! I only remember the smell was pretty awful. From our two or three rose bushes in the garden, he tried rose leaves and petals, dried and crushed. His favourite brand was from his own tobacco plants, which he grew in our tiny glass porch. If I remember rightly, he had to keep lighting up all the time. He was not a happy man though because his only pleasures, rabbit shooting and smoking his pipe, were gone.

Many tomatoes were available in season and apparently 30 tons of puree were made. The charge was 3 1/2d if you had a bottle and cork with you. At one time, turnips were quite plentiful for a time so the housewives would make jam. This was good to put over the potato skins which I remember well.

Queuing in Smith Street. I'm wearing white socks and shoes, with Joyce just behind me....

... and around the corner, still queuing at Collins sweet shop in the Pollet, for the last sweet ration in 1941

Jam Recipe

1½ pounds turnips
1½ pint water
1 teaspoon carrageen powder from the chemist
1 cup raspberry cordial

Boil turnips until tender, then mince. Put back into water. Add cordial and carrageen moss and boil for five minutes. Put into jars and cover.

When parsnips were in season, a country boy, H. Le Page told me he was put off Parsnips forever, when as a big treat at Christmas, there was to be a parsnip Christmas pudding, but he was sick of it as he had had parsnip soup all week! He mentioned having no toys and no beaches to explore, so would pass the time by catching frogs and butterflies. However, he fell into the boiler pit and almost drowned. So much for his game, it was short lived!

We children were fortunate as we were given milk every day at school and in April 1941, a ration of chocolate came from France for us but Collins, the famous sweet shop in the town, ran out of sweeteners and sugar so it was also a last sweet ration we queued up for and cost 3 ½ d (until 1945).

An order came from the Germans in 1942 wanting 500 tons of potatoes during the season and on the 27th March, an order for 150 gents' bicycles and they wanted them by the next day, the 28th March. Apparently, Jurat Leale and Mr Falla together after a good deal of persuading got away with giving less of potatoes and of only 100 bicycles.

With no potatoes on ration, I have read what a local vicar was saying at this time. He said all the conversation of the Islanders during the short period was only of food! One well-to-do lady was thrilled when someone gave her two potatoes, one big and one small. She looked at them lovingly but her conscience got the better of her at the last moment and she felt she should give one to her servants. She gave the large one and kept the small one. On enquiring if they enjoyed their lunch, with tears in their eyes, said 'When we opened it, the inside was all bad!' So much for giving and for being kind. This was probably the time Joyce and I began our "game" of potato gathering! (In the next chapter).

Whenever limpets were brought to market, queues would be sometimes two to three hours and always have to take your own wrapping paper for any fish. Limpets were really tough and would need much beating and cooking.

Mum and everyone else would try anything when it came to tea. Carrot, parsnip and sugar beet mixed with bramble leaf was tried, also green pea pods and blackberry leaves. Bramble leaves were on sale at 8d a pound.

I often think what a shame my mother hadn't kept the recipes of the time. It would have made interesting reading but really her time was too precious then, and also my fathers who helped with chopping the vegetables every evening for the meal. It was difficult to grow anything in the town.

On a meatless day, there was a letter printed in the Press which said to include octopus to recipes. They could be found in shallow waters at Bordeaux Harbour. Some brave Islanders looked for 'ormers' amongst the rocks on the beach at low tide but they unfortunately trod on mines and were killed. As early as 1941, beaches were out of bounds, but 5 young men in their twenties and thirties went out in a dinghy, hoping to find ormers on the south coast beaches, despite knowing no-one was allowed to step on land there because of mines. Whilst at Saints Bay, the German guard on duty fired a warning shot, so they quickly got back in the dinghy and rowed towards Moulin Huet, but the boat capsized and sadly three of the men drowned. One of them left a wife and 9 children. 'Mines eventually laid in Guernsey around the Island numbered 66,590'. Islanders were also warned not to be on the seaside area because of gun fire. So many places out of bounds!

2013, out of bounds only this past week was around the area of our lovely bluebell wood in St Martins, where a large sea mine was detected by chance by the Guernsey Police. The Canadian Airforce had dropped 74 of these mines way back in 1944 which weighed almost a ton and was 12 foot in length. It contained 850lbs of explosives. All dropped within a week just after the d day landing in June 1944, where most were dropped in the sea around the harbour district. Six landed on the island, one was detected a few years ago in 1996 also in the Bluebell wood, but three landed in our area of the town. One in Truchot Street, one at St George's Hall and another at the Royal Hotel. All places and roads I have mentioned in this book and it has been a reminder of me visiting 'Grangeclaire' almost opposite our house where myself and others could see this very large crater in the back garden of the next door house being 'Olinda'. I can't remember when this happened but the occupation archivist Mr John Goodwin mentioned that there was one mine still unaccounted for and seeing the other mines were more or less in a straight line to our home, it could well have been the one missing of the six.

18th of August 2013: Many residents who were living in the vicinity, were advised to vacate and leave their homes at 6am and 8am as the mine would be transported down to Fermain Bay to the sea. The Royal Naval Explosive Ordnance Disposal Officers and the Guernsey Police together successfully detonated the 'parachute' bomb where hundreds watched the explosion. Certainly a moment of Guernsey's history! Amazing that for almost 70 years it had laid in the famous beauty spot where over the years thousands of islanders and visitors had walked nearby.

Games which annoyed Otto and Hamel

When especially potatoes were short and with German stores situated at Le Truchot, just a short walk from home, it did not take long for my sister and I to take a shopping basket and our pram and hopefully go to find a few potatoes lying around the pavement. The boat would bring in potatoes for the forces and was brought loose from the harbour in lorries and horse and carts. The Guernseymen would unload them into the large wicker baskets on their backs and carry them into the large stores. They had to be careful, so had we, because the two Germans in charge were always shouting at us to 'Raus! Raus!' In other words, 'Clear off!' We did, but only for a minute or two! Otto and Hamel were large Germans. Hamel we always thought had been a boxer because he had a flattened nose and a cauliflower ear! The other one, Otto, I found out before my last book recently by workmen who knew him at the harbour was known as 'Bullneck'. Good name for him we thought. Hamel was called "Booter" by islanders who worked at the store. Bill Gillingham, who wrote his memoires for me in "A Time for Memories", was kicked if "Booter" thought they were slacking, when carrying 100 weight of potatoes into the store. Although, they were apparently allowed to take a few potatoes home each evening, which was a surprise to me.

Otto wore a khaki uniform and he was of the special German forces of the TODT organisation (we called them O.T.s), employed to control the slave labourers on the island. But he was also known to be cruel to the locals, and especially very cruel to the foreign workers at the harbour. We heard rumours of 30 slave labourers being killed while working in a ship's hold at the harbour, when a bomb landed straight down the funnel during an air raid.

The White Rock Plaque

Le Truchot. Offices now occupy where the potato stores were and where wagons and lorries unloaded

After school and knowing potatoes had arrived, we would take our pram and basket and wait for potatoes to fall, either crouching under the wagons and horses' bellies to collect or rush before they rolled back into the stores. With the help of workmen, we would collect them from the gutters when they tilted the baskets for us.

Most days we would take our pram into a friend's house and just hope to almost fill a basket and then happily transfer them, taking them home which really pleased our mother. But she was not pleased when I arrived home one day having been chased down Le Truchot and had a kick from Otto. I had a few tears and was holding my bottom and although it was my fault, standing on the step-board of the lorry, helping myself, dad felt I did not deserve this and was very angry with Otto. My father, who was also a tall man, said he would get Otto on Liberation Day and kill him! Every time he saw Otto pass in our street, he must have been boiling inside. He never forgave him but this did not stop us from carrying on with our little 'game' and there were several others who were still doing the same as us but I think we children got away with more than others. Joyce and I would also walk to other potato stores in the Charroterie and although the dark German bread had an awful flavour, we were occasionally given a slice with jam by a German soldier.

Always having a pram, we never missed a chance of filling it and on this particular day as we walked along the seafront, where a railway had been built to carry all the materials around the island for the fortifications, we spotted a large bag of cement in the road. With a shovel in the pram, we quickly collected the cement. The traffic did not worry us and we felt we had something that our father would be pleased with. From there, we

The train carrying materials around the island for the fortifications

would probably have been on our way to St George's wood store where the Guernsey boys knew us and would frequently hide bits of wood and shavings for us to collect. Germans were always present but they did not seem to mind us going there, not like the potato store and Otto and Hamel! A young German approached me there one day and offered me a loaf which I almost took until he spoke in German and I understood when he pointed to the stairs. I kept this to myself until 1985 when I mentioned it in my first book. If my parents had known, they would have barred us from going there but pleased to say I never saw him there when we went again.

At the old harbour, the boats would unload coal and one day walking past, Joyce and I noticed some lumps on the rocky sand, so not missing a chance again, we walked down the slipway and collected some coal in our pram. Soap was in very short supply during the Occupation so I dare say our mother was not too pleased to see us so black. Dad hardly recognised us when he saw us in the street later, and he told us never to venture there again – it was certainly "verboten"!

'OT's' The organisation Todt worked and guarded the Russians together with foreign slave workers on Guernsey.

Entertainment: The Finigan Sisters

We had much happier times and Joyce and I were dancing together as The Finigan Sisters during the shows of 1943 and up to June 1944. One show we were asked to dance in we chose red, white and blue material for our costumes, but that did not come off. I wonder why? It was amazing how attractive costumes were made to look with odds and ends of material which probably hadn't seen daylight for years. Also, a lot of parents who had children away were only too pleased to loan or sell their daughter's dancing clothes from when they danced before the war. With Germans always sitting in the front rows, it is strange that I could sing and dance "When the Guards are on Parade", and "The Kings Horses.." and then "All the Nice Girls love a Sailor" in a troupe, with no reaction from them, but they took exception to the singing of "Kiss me Goodnight, Sergeant Major". It was banned because it lacked dignity!

The Variety Shows we performed in were held mainly at Candie Gardens (then an Auditorium), the Lyric Theatre, the Central Halls and the old North Cinema. Sadly, not one of these buildings remain as entertainment places and The Little Theatre (the old Central Halls) unfortunately was burnt down.

These variety shows and all entertainment put together for the locals were enjoyed very much and many excellent entertainers emerged. One in particular, as a comedian, was our dear Cyd Gardner. Everyone loved him, also Len Winterflood because they

At Candie Gardens, my sister on the left, our teacher (Joyce Ferguson), Lorraine Corbin and me.

both made us laugh – this was just what the doctor ordered.

Mind you, my father gave a hearty laugh one evening and it cost him 10 Marks! It was at the Gaumont Cinema in St Julian's Avenue (now no longer a cinema) and the only time I went to see a film with my father, or with anyone else for that matter. Placed down the centre was a long dividing pole – one section of seats for the locals and the other side for the German Forces. Occasionally they showed a feature film with English sub-titles. Before this film they would show a newsreel emphasising how their Forces were winning the war. All of a sudden my father was amused at the propaganda and started to laugh aloud. Directly, three of the six Germans who were always guarding the exit doors rushed forward and demanded a 10 Mark fine on the spot! An expensive visit and we never went to the Gaumont again.

At other times, Dad relieved his boredom by going up to our small attic room during light evenings, and sit, hoping he would hear the sirens at the

German Military Band playing at Candie Gardens with islanders listening

harbour, and watch the Germans scatter for shelter with our planes overhead, and perhaps even see the bombing at times. He so loved and appreciated having the view of the harbour. During the latter part of the war, we could often see the sky over France lit up at night with flashes of gun fire and could hear the distant rumbling of bombardment, sometimes quite strong.

Occasionally at Candie Gardens, islanders and soldiers would be entertained by a military band concert, and proceeds would be given to the German Red Cross.

Apart from seeing the very excellent plays that were put on and going to the Variety Shows, my mother's pleasure, when she could, was to play 'Whist' and 'Euchre' (a very popular Guernsey card game) at small drives that were held in the town and sometimes at Ozanne Hall. I often went with her for company and to watch, sometimes to play if needed to make up another table. One evening, whilst coming home through the town, usually before 9pm because of the early curfew, we saw a group of soldiers coming up the Pollet street and looking rather merry and staggering a little. All were laughing and enjoying themselves when suddenly one came directly up to my mother and dug a revolver in her chest! We were so frightened and just stood frigid. We did not say a word but held our breath until he decided to drop the gun

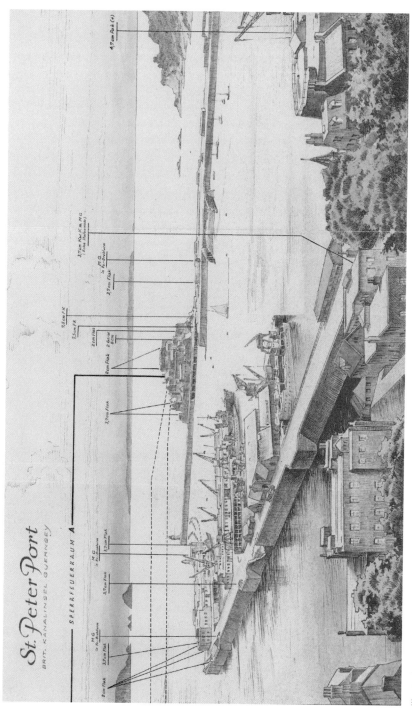

Illustration of the defences at St Peter Port Harbour - 1944 Festung Guernsey volumes *(Royal Court). View from Les Cotils.*

and place it back in his holster. He knew that he had frightened us and that is just what he wanted to do; with that, they merrily went on their way and so did we, although quite shaken by the experience. We almost ran home after this and the small whist drives missed our company for quite a while. After this incident, many older friends of my parents used to come home to play cards and if it was after curfew when they left, were pushed up over the garden walls to get home!

Recently, a friend, PC Simon Hamon came to visit me and said he had a photograph. He felt it was me at Candie gardens, from during the Occupation. I doubted it, but I was indeed surprised when he brought the photograph and yes he was correct. He had brought the album from America and the German who had apparently taken the photographs must have spent time in Guernsey during the Occupation, hence the photograph on Page 85 came to light after all these years.

Gaumont Cinema in St Julian's Avenue which are now offices. This cinema was a short stroll from my family home.

Threats and Deportation

Food was not the only worry, there were other concerns for Jurat Leale. He wrote in a booklet a preview of these eventful years and gave a speech. Following a successful commando raid by 2 local British Army soldiers in the first weeks of the Occupation, which resulted in our loss of wireless radios sets. The second landing a few weeks later brought fear as Jurat Leale wrote that the Germans threatened to shoot 20 leading Guernsey citizens unless they were satisfied that no-one was harbouring any British servicemen. The shooting did not take place but 17 islanders were imprisoned in Cherche Midi Prison in Paris for 2 months. Sadly one of them died of natural causes just days before the others were released. The submarine due to pick up the 2 soldiers could not do so, and eventually the 2 commandos gave themselves up and spent almost 5 years as Prisoners of War, where they were involved in many escape attempts.

In 1941-1942, the number of TODT slave workers reached maximum numbers. It was a very cold winter and no arrangements had been made for their arrivals. During 1943, contacts were made at the Red Cross because the prospects for potatoes and other food, clothing and footwear looked bleak. It was only later in July 1944 with the invasion of Normandy that the Red Cross message did get wirelessed to Geneva and help came.

You may be interested to read statistics and numbers kindly provided by Mr. Ken Tough of the Channel Islands Occupation Society.

FACTS & FIGURES ON THE OCCUPATION of Guernsey, the most densely populated and most heavily fortified Channel Island.

The Civilian Population

43,820 in 1939 in 24 square miles. 19,000 left for the UK including most men of military age and 4,700 schoolchildren. 23,981 civilians remained when the Germans arrived, including 1039 schoolchildren. War deaths were: 231 islanders in the British armed forces in all theatres of war, 30 in the German air raid on 28 June 1940, and 15 in allied air raids and mine-field accidents etc. 887 were interned in Germany.

The German Garrison

Maximum of 13,000 in May 1943, of whom 1850 were airmen and 1420 sailors, the latter being mostly flak and coastal artillery gunners respectively. There were more Germans per square mile in Guernsey than in Germany. 11,755 remained to be taken prisoner in 1945. 261 died during the Occupation, of whom 111 are buried in the British military cemetery at Fort George, Guernsey.

The Forced Workers

Maximum of 5,100 in May 1943, many from eastern Europe and north Africa. At least 97 are known to have died: 42 French, 15 Algerian, 10 Belgian, 10 Dutch, 6 Spaniards, 2 Polish, 1 Italian, 1 Chinese, 1 Russian, 1 Portuguese and 8 unknown. (This list is almost certainly incomplete and much research remains to be done).

The Fortifications

By September 1944, 272,000 cubic metres of reinforced concrete had been used in Guernsey, the majority in the spring and summers of 1942 and 1943. 74,746 mines had been sown along the 24 miles of coastline, 36 flak guns of 8.8cm, and 65 other heavier artillery pieces of up to 30.5cm calibre had been emplaced.

The Privations of the Civilian Population

The island imported an average of 16,636 tons of food annually prior to 1940. In the last nine months of the Occupation, when the islands were besieged by the Allies, no food could be imported. The adult weekly bread ration fell from 3lbs in November 1944 and no bread at all was available for three weeks from 13 February 1945. Petrol consumption fell from 108,000 gallons in May 1940 to 1872 gallons in April 1945. The population survived thanks to fortnightly issues of prisoner-of-war food parcels supplied by the International Red Cross.

There surely must have been an extremely worrying time during 1942 when deportation took place of grown-ups and children to a number of camps in Southern Germany for the duration of the war. This order shocked all Islanders.

All people of British birth, men, women and children were to be interned in Germany. This new law stated:

1 Persons now having their permanent residence in the Channel Islands.

2 All men not born in the Channel Islands and between 16 and 70 years of age, together with their families. (Unfortunately, some holiday-makers had been on Guernsey at the beginning of the Occupation and this applied to them too).

Many wondered why on earth elderly folk, women and children should also have to go. Apparently, five older people were so frightened, they took their own lives. Our family were indeed fortunate because we had all been born in Guernsey but one can understand the fear of leaving to go to an unknown destination after hearing so many horrible tales of the German camps. Notices were sent to those chosen on 18 September. They were to report to the old Gaumont Cinema in St Julian's Avenue, one group on 21 May and the second group on 23 September. On Guernsey, word got around easily and the parties concerned decided to have a 'do' before leaving but where at? The late Frank Stroobant who was also to be deported, author of 'One Man's War' was a popular owner of the then 'Home from Home' café on the seafront, decided it was to be in his cafe. He also managed to have food, sandwiches and drinks from different sources for everyone to have for the evening get together and also to take away with them, by asking in the newspapers and different Islanders such as growers and farmers who could help and give them a grand send off. With short notice, the evening came but Frank felt there might be trouble, so as a precaution, he prepared a short speech and it was translated into German, stating this was a final party of people who would be taken to Germany, and they would appreciate being left alone. The little speech did work with no interference even when the band started playing 'The White Cliffs of Dover', 'Land of Hope and Glory', 'There will always be an England' and 'Auld Lang Syne'.

Crowds of people collected outside until curfew time which was 10pm and over 200 voices sang loudly, especially the singing of 'Rule Britannia' and 'God Save the King'. The singing could clearly be heard at the Town Church! The Home from Home Cafe was situated at the Weighbridge near the Harbour Entrance. Many tears were shed that night but they all shared an evening they would never forget.

There was a delay in sailing due to the very rough weather but the boat sailed on 26 September and again, when leaving the harbour for St Malo, the singing on board was 'There will always be an England' and 'Rule Brittania'. These Islanders were mainly interned eventually in Biberach, Dorsten and Laufen. In all, 827 were deported in 1942 from Guernsey, and more followed in 1943. In all a total of more than a thousand.

When some evacuees and those deported to Germany returned to the Island during 1945/1946, they were unable to live in their homes and some had literally no homes left at all as 300 had been totally demolished. Friends and relations offered accommodation, mum and dad helped out a friend, Edie Masterton and her daughter Betty, whilst another daughter and husband, Jim Masterton, lived temporarily elsewhere. Betty and I slept together and although similar in age, she was far more advanced in every way than I was after living in the UK for five years. Naturally, the evacuees and deported, wanted to return as soon as possible but accommodation had to be found first and they were advised to bring all furniture and household equipment home (if any) they had accumulated whilst they were away.

I remember very well the Kitchenham family, also back from the UK, husband and wife and seven children, who came back and were accommodated at a large Esplanade house and had meals at the Hotel de France as it was called then, in La Plaiderie, and there were many other families staying there waiting to be housed. There were over 6,000 items of furniture collected from different homes, identification was difficult but many items were returned to their rightful owners. More explained in 'Reflections of Guernsey'.

My father, a builder with a small business, was kept very busy after

Liberation when materials started to arrive and priority was given to all those who were in the trade to come back earlier to help get Guernsey ship shape again. Hence Mr Kitchenham returned early and came to work for my father as he was a plasterer.

Within a short while in 1945, many salesmen from the UK were arriving in Guernsey wanting business as there were many items of every kind needed for work, renovating and repairing properties etc. I know my father welcomed a Mr Austin from Bristol. He told my father of a young friend (aged 14) who would like to have a pen friend, and since I was of the same age, would I like to write to her? Well, Joan Davis (as she was then), but now a widow Joan Hughes, still lives in Bristol and we are still friends and writing to each other after 68 years! We have only met for an hour or so when Joan and her mother came to Guernsey in the 1950s during a day trip from Jersey. Special memories and friendships of 1945 are still remembered to this day.

Foreign workers on the march

Internment, Deportation and Guernsey's Underground News Service 1942 & 1943

It was most difficult to try anything against the Germans although there were acts that one did get away with from time to time – hence the reason why the prison was forever full with waiting lists! In a published book 'Guernsey Green' by William Bell, I noted with interest that Bill Green did get away with it at times and he and his friends tried to form a 'resistance' group. But with second thoughts it was almost impossible to do anything as really there was nowhere to hide and if caught, serious reprisals would be taken on themselves and all the family, even on the Islanders. The small group that had met had to squash the idea. I remember very well the letter 'V' seemed to appear on many houses where Germans were living. Mostly, they were painted on, others were placed on walls and pillars in tar or bitumen.

Our own Special Constables were sent out with buckets and sponges to clean and clear up. 'V's (for Victory) were also cut out of paper and cardboard and left in places to annoy the Germans. Some were left and placed on car seats for the Germans to find on returning. They were dropped in streets, left on shop counters, slipped into folded newspapers and pushed through letter boxes of houses occupied by Germans.

ATTENTION—WARNING

Any persons found marking walls with 'V' signs or insults against the German Armed Forces are liable to be shot.

A reward will be paid to any persons giving information that will lead to the arrest of these offenders.

G. V. Schmettow
General,
German Military Government

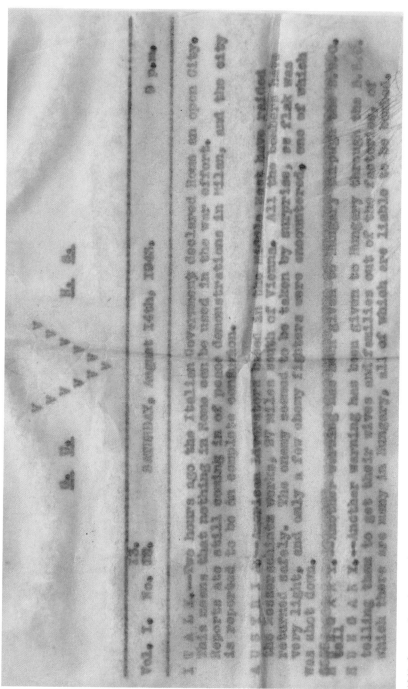

Vol. I. No. 38.   To   G.U.N.S.   SATURDAY, August 14th, 1943.   9 p.m.

I T A L Y.—Two hours ago the Italian Government declared Rome an open city. This means that nothing in Rome can be used in the war effort. Reports are still coming in of great demonstrations in Milan, and the city is reported to be in complete confusion.

A U S T R I A.—Swiss-Austrian frontier closed in the sole area have raided the aerodromes works, 27 miles east of Vienna. All the bombers have returned safely. The enemy seemed to be taken by surprise, as flak was very light, and only a few enemy fighters were encountered, one of which was shot down.

H U N G A R Y.—Counter-warning has been given to Hungary through the A.R.P. telling them to get their wives and families out of the factories, of which there are many in Hungary, all of which are liable to be bombed.

1943, Guernsey's underground news service was printed on thin tomato packing paper. (Image: Simon Hamon).

Acts like this annoyed the enemy and a reward of £25 was offered for the conviction of anyone committing these offences, but also could be shot!

Unfortunately, one Guernseyman was sentenced to five months imprisonment for being caught and he finished his term of sentence in 'Laufen' Internment Camp. Another man (besides other deeds done in the Cobo and Grandes Rocques districts) was sentenced to one year's imprisonment for chalking 'V's on the cycle seats of Germans' motorbikes whilst the soldier was drinking in hotel bars. The 'V' signs could be clearly seen on the seats of their trousers and were not easy to rub off until the trousers had been removed! Much teasing and laughter from their colleagues but most were very angry! Apparently, 19 children from the Castel parish school were also accused of having written 'V' signs in their districts and together with their parents and teachers were questioned before a German tribunal. They were dismissed with warnings, some 'fatherly' advice was given and threats of more serious consequences should it happen again. Also some children from our school, The Intermediate, did exactly the same with no consequences.

Some others were not so fortunate but saying that, Ron Hurford is the first to admit he was a 'wicked devil' when younger. He was aged 17 –

The Town Prison was built in 1811 at a cost of £11,000 and closed in 1990 when a new one was built elsewhere

Ron Hurford with Richard Heaume (of the German Occupation Museum) in the cell where Ron was imprisoned

18 at the time when he got into trouble having a go at a German. He was working at a local bake house at the time and certainly went a bit too far (we knew him well later as our friendly daily milkman!) He took the blame for his working mates who had stolen bread from the Germans and in the heat of the moment, he hit out and suffered physically and still shows the signs from the German blows to one of his eyes. He was also suffering mentally at the time. First, he was placed in the Guernsey jail and had to wait four and a half months for a trial. He was then sentenced to six weeks solitary confinement which to a young man must have been pretty daunting. Later, he was sent to Laufen Internment Camp. It was only recently I heard of the traumatic time he suffered and although finding it difficult to speak of his experiences and at what cruelty he had seen at times at Laufen, he felt like others who defied the enemy, the story should be recorded for posterity in the archive records of the C.I. Occupation Society.

The last V sign badge produced by Alf Williams *(Graham Williams)*

Whilst he was in solitary, Ron had no comfort whatsoever – no bed, only wood slats on the floor. He was allowed just one blanket as a covering for one night out of four, nothing else (like he said, it was a good thing he took in his 'Guernsey' with him). For three days, his ration of 2oz dry bread and coffee only was given. On the fourth day, he was allowed a normal day's ration, consisting mainly of watery soup and his blanket! In some ways, although very frightened I'm sure, I suppose he was relieved to see daylight and travel on the old cattle boat to St Malo, then on to Laufen Camp. There he still maintained his high adventurous spirit and was always in trouble for a further three years until the Camp was liberated by the Americans.

There were other islanders who punched and struck the Germans and were severely punished in prisons. One man, working for the Germans, showed his fist and for that he received 12 months in prison. Another brave Guernseyman, Mr Roy Machon, a projector operator at the Regal Cinema, started converting English silver coins into V sign brooches which featured the King's head inside a V. Hundreds of these were made and worn on the reverse side of coat lapels, but eventually the Germans caught up with him and he was tried and sentenced to 6 months imprisonment to be served at a Munich prison. He did so, then he was subsequently sent to the Laufen internment camp where many of the thousand or so islanders (Guernsey and Sark) were sent at this time. They were mostly English-born or "trouble-makers" who had offended against Occupation laws. The majority were deported to Biberach, but other camps included Dorsten, Compiegne, Kreutsberg, Liebenau, Wurzach and of course Laufen where Ron and Roy met up and became friends.

Another young Guernseyman escaped the net and carried on making brooches on a reduced scale – out of sixpences, florins and half-crowns. He was lucky not to get caught.

Because we had no radio sets, from June 1942 (and previously for over 3 months in 1940) and five brave men decided to form an underground organisation who made it their business to circulate the BBC news around the island (June 1942 – February 1944) and was known as GUNS: Guernsey's Underground News Service. The news sheets, which were printed in thin tomato packing paper, were handed to trusted friends but unfortunately, did eventually get into the wrong hands and these men were reported to the Gestapo with serious consequences. From the UK on May 8th 1945, one man who arrived was working with the M15 who was given a list of men who had helped the Germans throughout the occupation and amongst the list was a southern Irish man in his early 30s. During the evening he was arrested in Victoria Road, St Peter Port following a drunken disturbance. He was placed in prison just after midnight but apparently he escaped but he was found at home and was returned to prison. He was a collaborator and he had reported 'GUNS' and gave all details to them. Unfortunately he had been trusted as a friend and gave the daily news to the Germans. `GUNS' was conceived by Mr Charles Machon who sadly died in Hameln-Weser Hospital on October 26 1944 after being transferred from Potsdam prison, also Joe Gillingham did not survive. The other three men concerned were sentenced and were at Frankfurt prison for two months, then were transferred to the much grimmer prison at Naumberg, south of Liebzig. Details of 'GUNS' in Frank Falla's excellent book, The Silent War.

'GUNS', or Guernsey's Underground News Service, was not the only news sheet that was circulated during the Occupation. GASP, or Guernsey Active Secret Press, was probably more successful during this time as news was printed and distributed right up to Liberation Day and even reported Winston Churchill's speech and the King's message. Ludovic E Bertrand was the originator and editor of GASP, and it was circulated to local and foreign workers mainly through T. Moullin's Cycle Shop. It became a very busy shop with many cycles having problems! A word of caution was given to Mr Bertrand by Detective Inspector Banneville: "Go easy, this shop is being talked about too much, as it is the place to get real news".

Many 'agents' helped with the distribution and in particular, Mr Irvin Sims who was a printer for the 'Star' newspaper, and his wife Madeleine (whom I knew well later) worked at the Bailiff's office so she was in a position to pass on the news to the island officials, and also to the Bailiff. Another agent was the matron of our then Emergency Hospital, who believed that good truthful news would cheer up her patients (I am sure it did). Mr Bertrand took down the details of the BBC bulletins but there were several others who risked imprisonment and much worse like the brave group who also circulated 'GUNS'. More details about GASP in another excellent book 'Guernsey Occupied but Never Conquered' by William M. Bell.

The Guernsey prison was always full, and sometimes there was a long wait of several months before those sentenced were able to fulfil their time in prison. When civilians did not obey or tow the line, families would suffer. The German authorities would also carry out a very harsh punishment on their own members of the German Army if they were caught out of line. They thought themselves a disciplined and correct army and obeyed orders from the 'top dogs' to whoever deserved punishment, Islanders or fellow Germans.

Two Brave Women Imprisoned

Green

Mrs Winifred Green: 'Winnie' (as my mother, father and neighbours called her) lived in Les Canichers near us in a house called 'Psycho'. She had bravely got into trouble with a particular German working at the Royal Hotel during 1941. My mother had worked alongside her as a waitress before the war at the Hotel and knew her very well as she and her husband Frank lived only 3 doors away from us. Her two children had evacuated, so in wanting to fill time, she continued working there, whereas my mother did not.

Every morning, the greeting would be from a German, "Good morning Mrs Green, Heil Hitler". Mrs Green would answer, "Good morning, Heil Churchill!" Meals were eaten in the staff room but there must have been tense times for all the staff because at meal times the Germans would often mention to Mrs Green "Have you heard the news Mrs Green? We've got the Hood." (HMS Hood). A few days later, Mrs Green got her own back. Looking at the German, she said "Heard the news? We've got the Bismarck!" This continued and I'm sure my mother would have been kept up to date as to what was going on between them. Then, one lunchtime, the German asked "Would you like some rice pudding Mrs Green?" Yes please came the answer, but the reply was "only if you say Heil Hitler"! The other workers in the room expected something of an answer, but surely not this. "To hell with

A special occasion dinner at the Royal Hotel, post war. My mother 1st left and Winnie 3rd from the right.

Hitler for a rice pudding – and one made with skimmed milk at that!" This remark obviously angered the German more. It was on October 13th 1941 that police called for Winnie Green at the hotel, and she had to go with them and was in court at 11am. No-one defended her and it was all in German, although it was translated to her by an interpreter. She admitted to what she had said regarding the rice pudding, and was sentenced to six months imprisonment in Caen, France. Frank knew nothing of this, so naturally Winnie was worried. She eventually had permission to call on him with an escort, but decided to go straight to jail as she did not want neighbours to see her.

It was later that two nice young Germans broke the news to Frank about the trouble and her jail sentence.

She spent two weeks in the Town (St Peter Port) prison before being marched down to the boat. Winnie spent five days at Granville prison in a cell with French prostitutes who were kind to her, and like she said, showed sympathy towards her. Eventually Frank wrote to the prison authorities and explained Winnie had no defence at her trial. With that she was allowed to come home earlier, which she was grateful for as she had endured a very uncomfortable time in the cells she shared with others at Caen.

She was at Caen for 4 months. Two sisters from Jersey were with her there. Their crime was making 'V' for victory signs. (I wrote about the V signs in 'A Time for Memories'). The Jersey sisters and Winnie got on very well together and they would keep up their morale by making up their faces every day. They had no privacy. There were no screens and the sanitary bucket was chained to the wall and was never cleaned. They all kept cheerful despite this and also with the lack of baths and shortage of water. They were allowed only one and a half pints of water each a day. They would even strain the bits of cabbage out of their 'soup' and use the water to wash their feet! The worst thing according to Winnie, was the sanitary bucket in the cell, and the best and most important was the calendar each prisoner made for themselves out of scrounged bits of paper. Every morning each one would cross that day off, even though they had to live through it.

Winnie managed to borrow a needle and thread from another prisoner and tore a piece of her sheet, which she embroidered with 'Heil Churchill. RAF Caen Prison 1941'. She managed to bring it home, sewed between the linings of her coat. She was certainly lucky not to have been caught with it.

With having plenty of free time, which she hated, they made playing cards out of cardboard and played 'snap' and other games.

Winnie eventually said goodbye to her Jersey friends, but she felt sorry to think they still had several more months to serve. When she came back, she worked again at the Royal Hotel, where she was known as 'Mrs Churchill'. I am sure my mother and Winnie would have had lots to talk about when she returned. Frank (her husband) was frequently at home too, as he was the plumber of the district.

Major Marie Ozanne

There was another brave Guernsey lady who risked her life opposing the German forces and who was imprisoned by doing so. She was Miss Marie Ozanne, a Salvation Army officer, who was recently recognised for her brave actions during the Occupation. She was a devoted member of the Salvation Army and she would preach to the Islanders in the town markets during 1941 and 1942 and objected strongly regarding the closing down of the Salvation Army on Guernsey (the Germans were against and stopped the wearing of all uniforms of any kind). She was also against the bad treatment

and persecution of the Jews and of the organisation TODT forced labourers on the Island and the deporting of UK born Islanders. There was a house named "Paradis" approximately half a mile from her home in the Vale, and it was a prison for Organisation Todt foreign workers. She heard the screams from these men and she therefore objected strongly and wrote directly to the German authorities despite knowing she could be arrested for doing so. This was a very serious offence and eventually she was imprisoned for directly confronting the Germans. Sadly, after six weeks in prison and a period in hospital, Miss Ozanne's health deteriorated and she died soon afterwards in 1943, a young woman. The Salvation Army has now (February 2013) recognised her contribution and together with the Ozanne family, has sponsored 'the blue plaque' which was placed on Major Marie Ozanne's former home in the Vale by Guernsey's Bailiff, Mr Richard Collas. She was certainly a very brave lady and richly deserved the recognition by the Salvation Army which awarded her posthumously its highest honour 'The Order of the Founder'. This was the Island's fourth blue plaque honours on Guernsey to be unveiled but Miss Ozanne was the first lady to be honoured in this way.

Intermediate School

We children soon got used to seeing the many uniformed soldiers around in St Peter Port, and we soon settled at school with new friends. I was at Vauvert School for two years which opened very soon into the Occupation, but the Intermediate School did not open until April 1941 with only 68 boys and girls for two days a week only. By September, it was possible to open on a third day, but not for long as the German troops commandeered the school building in November 1941, and the authorities were very concerned about the move. The President of the school, Canon E. L. Frossard, was

I am walking past an entrance gate at Notre Dame School (and Occupation Intermediate)

relieved as he received an offer of help from the Germans, saying they would give assistance as they wanted the move to be on that same day. Surprising, well the help came! One soldier holding each corner carrying the load of materials, papers etc. to the door, and just dumped everything in the playground in a heap. It was wise that Mr Girard salvaged everything, and arrangements were made for the 'Glasshouse' workers to come and bring lorries to collect every item. For many weeks afterwards, many groups of ladies were sorting out pens, pencils, books, rulers, paint boxes etc. so that the school could open as soon as possible at the Notre Dame School in Burnt Lane.

The school was open for three full days every week and during this time, the nuns and kind sisters of the Church provided a soup and vegetables cooked in a bakers oven (see later). Mr Girard, our headmaster, decided this arrangement was best as when checking the children's lunches brought in, one child would only bring in a meal of fried potato peels. So at least he felt we had a nourishing meal on the three days of school. Tuesdays, Thursdays and Saturdays were half days so it was probably then we could help at home or go scrounging! As time went by, Mr Girard found it very difficult to obtain vegetables and beans for the soup kitchens he had organised. Cobo Butchers supplied bones and at times, if they could, they would leave a little meat with them.

From mid-1943 to Liberation, apparently 21,000 meals had been enjoyed from the soup kitchens. When in 1945, not having bread for three weeks and no vegetables available, it was thought the kitchens would close down, but prayers were answered at the last minute when two gentlemen (Jurat J. Allez and Mr C. Moullin) telephoned and offered the schools, ten tons of vegetables that were destined for the Germans! They knew of the importance of these for children and took risks in hiding them in a very special place. It was not only Mr Girard who was concerned for us children, as his father worked and collected the tons of vegetables by horse and cart, and hid them all, then set about peeling the small pig potatoes with a peeler rescued from a scrap heap. There were many people responsible in helping the food supply throughout the five years, especially if it could reduce the food for the Germans.

The highlight of the day was queuing for our dish of bean soup which the

The man who found a potato in his soup!

Soup and potatoes. It was beans we looked for!

kind nuns had prepared and cooked. We queued very orderly and when our turn came to be in the front all our attention was on the person in front of you, holding the bowl out, and just hoping the ladle was not lowered too much with either the girl or boy acquiring all the beans from the bottom! Families living in the town just could not buy vegetables easily so having a nice home-made vegetable soup three times a week was a luxury and something we all looked forward to. We had the Headmaster, Mr Peter Girard, to thank for getting us those precious beans and vegetables.

I can understand why Mr Girard had remarked "it is not a happy time to be a headmaster", and his concern when checking the 44 children that stayed at school over lunchtime: 24 had only one slice of bread, 14 had half a slice and 6 had no bread at all. We had a lot to be thankful for, as I always looked forward to the soup the nuns (and Mr Girard and others) provided for us at the Intermediate, just like the pupils of Castel, Cobo, and Hautes Capelles Schools. Communal cooking also came into being towards the end which

A SPY AT SCHOOL

Going back to the worry & concern of teachers throughout the 5 years, most concern was felt by mr Peter Girard (Headmaster of our school – The Intermediate) during the early part of the Occupation. Writing his Memoirs after the war (mainly connected with our education) he was approached & introduced to a German Civilian by the Guernsey Education Council as a School-Master anxious to improve his knowledge of English. He wished to be allowed to 'sit-in' at lessons given at the school. mr Girard felt this was reasonable enough until he was unofficially informed by a member of our local Guernsey Police Force that this man was thought to be a member of the 'Gestapo'. From then onwards everyone was very careful with any conversation when he was about.

After a time he sought permission of the Education Council wanting to give lessons to the more advanced pupils, who eventually enjoyed taking part in plays he organised. Even though he seemed a pleasant man, he was treated with caution & there was a time when mr Girard felt most uneasy watching boys thoroughly enjoying themselves pelting him with snow-balls!

It was some 10 years after the Liberation & Occupation had ended that mr Girard received a letter from the German admitting he was a member of the 'Feldgendarmerie' (German Police) at the time, but also assured mr Girard he had no reason whatsoever to report him (nor us!) whilst at the school.

1942 ??   1941

107

helped many.

One of our teachers was Miss A.A. Moon at the Intermediate, quite a big but short lady. She seemed quite elderly to us, but probably wasn't. She was often seen with her pram collecting twigs and if lucky, a few small branches. When she entered our classroom, it was always with a loud "Wake up please!", then we had to sit up straight and listen. She was a good teacher and I liked her very much. Not all teachers were so popular.

At the Intermediate School the German Language had to be taught and naturally had to be a very important lesson. We had several long lessons every week. The German lessons were compulsory from January 1942 when children reached 12 years of age. Our daily newspapers printed sentences in German and English daily to encourage all readers to learn.

There was one incident that must have caused Mr Girard and the School Committee some embarrassment and concern. At one stage two senior girls wanted to be excused from learning the Language as they were preparing for their 'School Certificate' and felt that time spent on learning German was wasted as they were not including this subject in their Exam. This they were allowed to do, but then a little later on the other scholars in their class decided they too did not want to learn German either and they, being determined, felt very strongly about giving it up!

This refusal by the pupils must have caused some difficulties with the German Authorities as I am sure Mrs Tate, our German teacher, would have had to report any serious disruptions such as this. With discussions all round, this was happily sorted out and the class resumed with the "Deutsch".

The outcome must have pleased our teacher, Mrs Tate, who was German herself and who indeed was a very fiery character and who definitely would not have liked being put out in any way!

I can well remember being questioned by a German Officer who used to visit the school quite regularly (but not too often, glad to say) to check on our progress. He used to stand in front of the class and just point at random and showed much pleasure when answered correctly in the German language. There was always a Prize every year for the scholar with high marks, also at one Prize Giving two German Officers were present and we were taught a special German song that had to be included during the Ceremonies. Good second-hand books were given out as prizes and we were grateful and pleased if we received one. The School Committee did their very best for us always.

Pupils came from all over the Island and seeing there was no transport for them, they either had to walk or cycle to school. Everyone on the island seemed to have a cycle, where they came from was a mystery. A lot of them at school had been made with many spare parts and bits and pieces, others hadn't seen daylight for years I'm sure. We used to laugh at our friends' cycles for when the tyres needed to be replaced, hose pipes and ropes were bought to be used together to form a 'tyre'. This of course was a very bumpy ride for the scholars, some had to come from the Forest, or St. Saviours, but it was funny for us to watch them go off k-clump k-clump along the road! One can imagine this I'm sure. I'm sure many of the country children like us were quite pleased as in 1944, and after D Day with the bombing raids of the Allies near town, authorities decided to close our school from May through to the end of August.

One of the main interests at school during the occupation was reading the Leaflets that were brought into the school on the quiet. These leaflets with up-to-date news of the war were dropped in the Country by British planes and brought in by the boys and girls and shown around the classroom.

All of the reports were true information on how the war was progressing and we used to feel so important going home and giving the family all the latest news and also telling the tales how the leaflets found their way to school. It was mainly the boys who used to bring them in as they would clamber into fields, over hedges and up trees if they spotted anything resembling paper. One such boy, Tom Jehan, who was in my class, did just that. One day he climbed up high into a tree to get the Leaflet, struggled to get there and then clambered down to get on his bike but also found a German Officer was waiting for him below! There was nothing else for him to do but to get down and hand over his prize! We can laugh about it now but at the time it was frightening for Tom.

All this time the teachers were very understanding and if I remember rightly

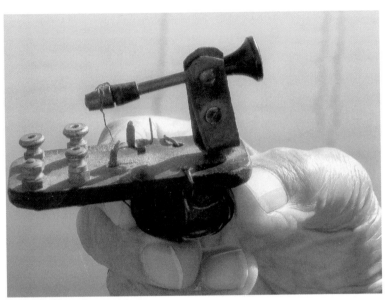
Roy holding his precious crystal set

did not push us too hard. Strangely enough, it was only our German female teacher who had a very quick fiery temper and who did! Many ex-pupils I am sure will remember her and the book hitting our heads and many other items being thrown at us! The headmaster and all the other teachers made up for her though and we had many kindnesses and much help from them.

In one file of the Education Council are details of the time when a parent wrote complaining that a teacher at the mixed Intermediate School had shown 'brutality' for no civilized reason towards his daughter. The teacher promised that she would not hit children again, especially across the head. Many who were at our school would surely guess right who the teacher was.

I can only speak generally of school years and from when I passed the scholarship to the Intermediate School from Vauvert, the teachers and the Education Committee did their utmost to make our time at school as happy as possible, and even one of our teachers Mr Dowding affectionately known as 'Dido' by the boys, who risked imprisonment (or possibly more) by teaching the older boys how to make the forbidden crystal sets! News of the war and of the UK was so important to islanders then and many crystal sets were made. I have spoken recently to Roy Falla, who was a teenager then, who listened regularly to a crystal set he made which measured 2.5 inches long by 1 inch wide, being so small it could easily be hidden should Germans be around. Roy said he made several for different people and he was never caught. (More about that in my book, A Time for Memories).

Many hundreds of crystal sets were made and thousands of people, like Roy, would listen to the BBC every day.

I often used to pop over to friends who lived opposite, 'Aunty Elise' and 'Uncle Stan' Delamothe, who had a crystal set in their bedroom. I used to love fiddling with the 'whisker's' and listen to the news, and sometimes when I felt safe would listen to music. One day I looked out of the window to the garden below and there watching me was a German soldier! I was scared and quickly took the earphones off as he must have realised what I was up to. Gladly I never saw him again or heard anymore, I was just very careful the next time I popped over.

A familiar sight on my way to school. German soldiers in the Town's High Street.
There was almost one German to one civilian during the occupation at different periods.

Diary of a Night-time Central Telephone Operator

I have written in a 'A Child's War' and previously of a German sitting in class 'perfecting his English', but his real intentions was to report back to headquarters anything suspicious that the children or teachers might say. He was one of the Military Police. Files have also revealed that apparently, there were 30 Gestapo secret police in plain clothes walking around Guernsey living and working amongst us in unknown jobs. German women and guards were stationed at the Central telephone exchange in the Grange, St Peter Port.

Here follows extracts from a diary, kept by Miss Elsie Windsor who was a night time telephone switchboard operator there.

1940

June 28th 1940 - In perfect weather three German planes flew over the White Rock. Two rows of produce waiting shipping. Crowds of people watching. They bombed all the produce, people rushed to the New Jetty. Being a low tide they took shelter underneath which saved about 200 from being killed. Three houses in the Strand were hit, several people were sheltering in the cellar, not one hurt, but 90 people injured in the one raid with 34 killed.

September 24th - English planes flew over in the early hours of the morning. They dropped leaflets with a message from the King and Queen and a picture of both of them standing in the ruins of Buckingham Palace. I was lucky to get one. The RAF dropped 10 Daily Mirrors as well.

November 7th 1940 - Sitting at work when a big tap on the door. Two big fish-face, pug nose, looking for friends came in. After remaining 45 minutes, peeping into everything, then left the room. They thought we had some secret line to the mainland, but they were mistaken. They were private detectives.

Radios back for Christmas

Our wireless was returned to us after being taken from us for six weeks. We all had to suffer (Island fishermen had left in a boat for the UK), that was our punishment.

1941

March 18th 1941 - Telephone wires cut at the airport, so back the curfew goes to 9pm.

RAF bomb 1000 Germans. The BBC gave news that the RAF bombed a boat 50 miles off the Channel Islands. The boat left here with 750 Germans, called in at Jersey picking up another 750. We have not heard from the Germans since the boat was sunk.

July 6th 1.15am & September 18th - English planes over Guernsey. Bombs dropped somewhere in Pleinmont. The anti-aircraft guns were soon in action. Fireworks display, gee, what a noise, even mother heard it ('apparently she had hearing loss') We had a thrill.

Winter: No coal or wood is sent out to us. We have tickets for coal also wood. One hundred weight a month, only a shilling worth of gas a week for cooking and lighting, so we will have to go to bed at 5pm. One candle a month on ration.

1942

Jan 1st 1942 - Leading some friends. Spent a quiet day, beautiful weather, very mild. A friend brought us two pounds of potatoes or we wouldn't have had any as there are none about. Our "friends" have eaten them!

Jan 9th 8.45am - Air raid with two endings. Just about to leave work when a British plane came over, then off went the fireworks again. We had to remain at work, heaps of shrapnel fell like hail on the roofs of houses around Victoria Road, Brock Road and The Grange. They said one of our planes was down seven kilometres from Guernsey, but on the wireless they said all returned to their base (so they're liars!)

February 14th - British planes over at 8.30pm. Germans put a very heavy gunfire but at 10pm we thought our exchange was blown up. The anti aircraft was dreadful, however, we are still here to tell the tale. The raid was over the town, could hear the shrapnel falling on the houses like hail, although my mother heard it very well.

August 18th - British landed on France, wireless news. Germans here had the wind up. All the exchanges were sent home.

August 19th - Germans took charge, everybody sent home. We didn't even have to go to work at night – whoopee, what a holiday! Never known this since the Exchange opened.

December 18th - Germans had another mock battle. We were chased out of our switchroom again and not allowed to return until 10.45pm. Everything was quiet. Hope the British haven't forgotten us.

December 25th - Not to be forgotten. The Germans allowed us a little more meat. We had a piece of beef, two potatoes for each person, like pig potatoes. Some walnuts came from France. I nearly got squashed to a sausage trying to stand in the queue for half an hour. Collins in the Pollet made Guernsey Sweets so we had 2oz each. It was a real treat to taste a sweet however. We had a very good dinner but our thoughts were in England all the day. I went to hear the Guernsey broadcast, but I was disappointed. We were all alone on Christmas Day thinking of you all.

1943

January 29th 1943 - Friends and I were at a play ('The Ghost Train') at the Central Halls when the British passed over. Gosh, what a noise, we could scarcely hear what was going on. We had thoughts of staying the night, but on night duty we managed to get to work by 8.30 ok. Then at 9.00am they came again, seen some ships, they dropped a bomb on one. It nearly shook the Exchange down. However, the boat was hit and is lying at the bottom of the Harbour. Eight killed and 13 wounded. Fireworks wasn't it, we do see life!

German soldiers came and took over the Exchange saying 'Alarm'. Took all the connections off the board, and we were sent home. Just had supper with mother who was quite pleased I was home to sleep, when I heard a knock at the door. When I answered two Germans were in a lovely car to fetch us back, they had made a mistake. We felt like saying something, but had respect for our men folk.

Big guns fired. All the town people had to evacuate, but not Victoria Road. The Town Hospital, the Prison and Police Station, everywhere was closed while they fired heavy guns and we had to leave all doors and windows open.

March 24th 1943 - Big Guns Fired

April 15th - British all over the island, very heavy gunfire, shrapnel came through our greenhouse.

April 16th – 21st - British over every day. Also over France. We hear all the bombardment over Cherbourg etc. Poor beggars, they don't get much peace.

April 24th - Sir Donald Banks spoke of Guernsey on the wireless, it was lovely to hear him.

Have been three weeks without sugar. Only 2lb potatoes allowed, one pound her head. Have not had any since 2 weeks before Christmas. Went to St Peters on foot to get 50 pounds. Friend came with me, had our lunch on a hedge, onion sandwich. We get only nine pounds of bread between us both and no flour, so we are not very fat.

I couldn't walk that far now, as we get too tired, having very little food. I worry everyday what to give mother to eat, our vegetables are very scarce. We have to make soup with some muck from France. Just been weighed, have lost two stone, two pounds. Looking forward to a treat tomorrow. Half a pound of dates arrived for each person. We paid nearly one shilling a pound for potatoes like the size of beads, and they were nearly all frost bitten, but we had to eat them. We have oats like the horses eat, also barley flour 6oz each. It smells so bad we have got to eat it or we'd starve. We got a lot to thank Hitler for.

German planes on their way to England cross here for the South West counties and get heavily bombed.

May 14th - Boats left here with troops. British planes came over, then heavy gunfire was heard, boats came back – 9 killed and 17 wounded. British over again on May 16th.

May 23rd - Sunday morning about 8.15, a convoy was coming in when British planes came over, gosh what a noise. They sunk two boats just outside the harbour and damaged two others. Eight killed and 15 wounded, several drowned. Our food boats not touched.

May 30th (my birthday) - No meat for three weeks. Five boats have been sunk this week around Guernsey. Saturday afternoon, what a row, but lovely to see them.

August 15th - Seven persons got away by boat. Very selfish my point of view, as we all had to suffer. No fishing has been allowed, and no-one has been allowed on the beaches. Nothing has been heard of them. Suppose they have arrived. One father was very worried, he didn't know his daughter was going.

August 20th - English planes chasing Germans over the Island. They hit their own *planes, bringing one down on the beach on Herm, one off Sark and another off Jersey. That was a good day's work. Gee, what a barrage they put up. It was about 8pm.*

August 29th - British planes over again and on September 4th. Suppose on their way to France.

September 7th - Blackberries.

September 8th - Very heavy firing somewhere in France, lasting 3 hours.

In November, bodies washed ashore from the Charybdis. Islanders sending 700 wreaths for the funeral. ('We children gave freely for a floral tribute also for the HM Cruiser Charybdis and abandoned school in hundreds to attend the funeral at the Foulon Cemetery, over 5000 Islanders attended')

November 16th - Heavy firing – British over again. Going to the funeral

December 29th - Unhappy landing on Sark. British tried a landing on Sark. Unfortunate for our boys, they got into a minefield and two were killed also one German wounded.

1944

January 7th 1944 - British plane passed over in the morning, then again at 2pm. Four German fighters and two British were over the sea, our boys had one plane down which fell at St Martin's Point. The other had to land as he was badly damaged. Our boys got away safe, they passed over our home.

March 5th -Two German planes came down, one in the sea and the other in the Castel parish fell into the trees, the pilot was killed.

May 27th - 100 injured in Fort George attack. Friend and I go out twigging in the Green Lanes when we heard a roar of planes coming. We thought it sounded like German planes, till we heard the siren go, then bangs. We took to our heels and rushed under shelter. Twenty of our planes came over the Fort, did a lot of damage to houses on the Fort Road, also at Fort George, they killed several Germans and over 100 wounded. They were playing football on the field.

On June 2nd = They came again. They dropped bombs on the Fort Road doing a good deal of damage, demolished one house completely, also wrecked three others. A lot of damage at the Fort, killing several. They come over the island every day. One came down over Sark.

June 3rd - Saturday night at 8.30pm. 40 Americans came over the Fort again, gee what a din. They dropped bombs on the Fort Road, a lot of damage again to the houses, all people to move out, no one injured. Mother was very nervous.

Sunday June 4th - They came again at 3.15pm.

June 5/6th - Germans came to the Exchange and turned us both out. The British had made a landing in France and hundreds of planes passed over our heads during the night. We were turned out and had to go home with an escort at 3.30am. Fancy walking home with a German, never thought I'd do that! Had my key so let myself in. Mother sound asleep with that din in the sky.

June 19th - American planes came over, dropped a large bomb in the old harbour which shook the whole town. Every shop in town, the Bordage and Mill Street were all with smashed glass. It was sad to walk through. The Town Church was smashed as well, all the shops were closed. This happened at 8.30 am, only one man was hurt in the chest. Wasn't it wonderful.

July 2nd - Germans gave us permission to go back to work. Four weeks closed. We can only enter with permits.

July 24th - British planes came over at 19.30 when three boats were just leaving the White Rock. They dropped bombs on one and sank it, split in half. Cries from sailors and soldiers could be heard as far away as the 'Halfway'. They also damaged the other two. Several killed on them. The bombs were heard all from home.

September 3rd - About 500 planes passed over Guernsey. The Germans popped at them, fire also and smoke coming out of one, but he was able to carry on. The Germans must have hit them. Gosh, what a noise, this was on Sunday morning about 9 o'clock.

December 27th - What a godsend. Our Red Cross ship arrived, crowds to see her, the people were excited, hundreds came from all over the island (country) to cheer her. It was a wonderful sight. Mother was very tearful. We had the worst Christmas we have had for many years. We had no gas, and very little wood. We had to take our dinner to the bake-house. We had a wee bit of pork but when I went to fetch it, we couldn't put our fork in the potatoes. Poor old Ma was in tears so we had to take it back and have our dinner for tea. We had carrots, parsnips and swede, and a few potatoes. Never mind, we hope it is our last. We had a little black market flour and a few apples so mother made an apple pudding for tea, so we had a swell tea and we will never forget it.

December 31st - We have just had our Red Cross parcels. What a thrill to see a piece of chocolate. We only get 3 pounds each of bread, so we are not very fat.

December 31st - 13 Canadian airmen were forced down at L'Ancresse. They lost their plane, the Germans saved them. All lived at Happy Landings Hotel. 2 more were picked up on New Years Day. They had bailed out and arrived in a rubber dinghy, also 2 bodies were washed ashore.

(During the five years of occupation, there were at least 139 air crew of allies forces perished in the Bailiwick of Guernsey, told to me recently by Richard Heaume, owner of the German Occupation Museum and John Goodwin the German Occupation Archivist, who has worked tirelessly for information and who continues with the research.)

1945

January 28th 1945 - Second issue of Red Cross parcels.

March 3rd - 3rd issue of Red Cross parcels (New Zealand), but longing to see the flour boat – expected on march 5th.

Mr and Mrs Siguart found dead. (Apparently they were shot by a German for food in a St Peter Port home).

End of diary.

Not knowing Miss Windsor, I have wondered if she had more knowledge of events by working at the exchange? She knew how very serious the consequences would be if caught keeping a diary, should the Germans find out. Maybe this is the reason that her writing was very very small as it was difficult to decipher. With sincere thanks to Mr. Michael Williams for doing so.

Renaut de Garis and The Mirus Battery

It was while talking to friends about old Guernsey characters still living on the island, that a gentleman in his 90s was mentioned, a Mr Renaut de Garis. It was recommended that I should talk to him and advised where I could find him every day – sitting in his car over-looking Lihou Island. I was promised an interesting conversation which was mainly of his Occupation memories, not all happy as I found out.

Mr Renaut de Garis

I arrived at L'Érée, situated on the west of the island, and sure enough, Mr de Garis was in his small blue car. Although a little surprised when I spoke his name, he welcomed a conversation (as we Guernsey 'Donkeys' do) and he welcomed me into the front of his car. Renaut was very alert and his memory was excellent, even at 98 years old, now soon to celebrate his 100th birthday. His love of the sea and the area he had always lived in, went back all his life and even at 14 years old, he had built a 14 foot flat bottomed boat and got hold of a motorcycle engine and made it fit. Hence he made many friends amongst the west coast fishermen and was popular. I gathered this from talking to him at another meeting, when I took a recording of his early life in Guernsey.

Renaut married Adèle in September 1939 and the happy couple moved into a newly built beautiful house in La Vieille Rue. He and his father owned a vast area of land and greenhouses and like many others, they were growers- until the German occupying forces arrived and their lives (like everyone else's) changed completely in a very short space of time.

Within weeks, high ranking German officers made several visits to the couple's home asking questions and looking around. Renaut and Adèle felt there was something big in their minds (you will read later how big!)

With living only seven months in their brand new home, the Germans ordered the young couple out and they had to leave everything in the home intact by the following day. It was very fortunate there was an empty house available just down the road called "Le Grand Douit" that they could move into, but they were very sad to leave.

This order to leave their homes, as you have read happened to many islanders, one can imagine how Renaut and Adèle felt towards the new occupying forces, especially as they were just married and settled in a newly built home.

There were over 2000 houses that were vacated in 1940 due to the evacuation and they were occupied by the German forces, the foreign workers or islanders that were evicted by the Germans. The homes that had been lived in (such as Renaut and Adèle's) were mostly left in a terrible state. Some had to be gutted due to so much damage. After Liberation, 3000 houses were in need of repair work, and at the time of the Liberation

1,373 houses were still being used by the Germans. Only a small number were left in a liveable condition. In many cases, fittings had been looted and owing to the fuel shortage during the last year, woodwork, doors and wooden floors, had been ripped out and used for fuel. My father, a builder, owned two cottages in the Green Lanes which the Germans had taken over. There was extensive damage for which he later received a little compensation.

The Hotel Beaulieu, St Martin's taken over as a Soldatenheim Soldiers Home staffed by nurses Klara and Ebba seen on the balcony. 1942. *(Paul Upton)*

Renaut remembers there soon being much activity in the area, and slave workers of all nationalities were seen coming and going. The TODT workers were having to live and work in terrible conditions with very little food and only rags for clothing. Renaut (like myself) remembers the cement bags that were their footwear. Some were luckier to have sacks under their feet.

A friend then informed Renaut that the roof tiles from his house and timbers were being taken away and transported to a hotel in St Martins parish (the former Hotel Beaulieu). The roads surrounding the airport and the area of Renaut's land were mined, so it was difficult and forbidden to see what was going on.

Eventually, a train and railway was built and materials were transported

Clockwise from top left: The construction of one of the four gun positions at Batterie Mirus. *(SH)*; The 100 ton floating crane ANTEE seen here after arrival from France, bringing the Mirus guns. *(John Goodwin)*; The slow movement of one of the Mirus gun barrels on a 24 wheeled trailer along L'Eclet where the hedge had been removed and a new road laid, to avoid the S bend in the Clos Landais *(CIOS)*; Camouflaged as a bungalow is 30.5 cm Mirus gun position number one *(CIOS)*

from the Harbour, towards the north of the island, then to Cobo, Vazon and Perelle, for the building of the island's fortifications and more than 800 bunkers in all were built around the island. Houses and glasshouses were demolished along the way to enable this to happen, and roads were widened to enable these large transporters to bring guns to the areas – especially on the land owned by Renaut's family.

These 4 large naval guns *(opposite)* were very elaborately fitted out and were placed in 4 fields (now known as the Mirus Battery), and when these great guns fired Renaut's vinery was smashed to pieces. His house and all his property and land were taken over. Because he and Adèle intended and hoped to return to their home one day, Renaut had to approach Commandant Mullen who lived in the house and who was in sole command of the Mirus Battery, for permission to employ workmen to collect the glass strewn all over the land. He said it was "just like snow" and took a long time to clear.

It wasn't until May 1945 when after Liberation, that the house could be seen and what a mess had been left. Apparently in 1941, the Germans had removed the top floor of the house altogether, all bay windows gone, and they had been in a lovely Columbian pine, also gone was the staircase in the same wood, and no fire places to be seen. Many forced workers had to build an outside staircase and a great steel roof one foot thick on which a 'pom pom' gun was mounted. Renaut found this out when the rebuilding began again, which he said cost three times as much as the original cost in 1939.

Floors and walls were also in reinforced concrete which one can understand as a large searchlight was also placed on the roof.

Internal damage was vast, like so many other German occupied houses, but Adele and Renaut felt their German presence more than most on his property. At L'Eree, the Germans had huge stone crushers for removal of the large shingle bank and sandbanks for building work, making a huge quarry. Both sides of the road were built in the 1600s and were badly damaged. This also upset Renaut seeing such damage to parts of historic Guernsey property being altered.

At least Renaut and his uncle got away with taking wooden sleepers that were ready to be placed in readiness for the German railway. They took several during the night-time at Perelle and buried them. The Gestapo came and searched but theirs were never found. Others were taken but Renaut never found out if the islanders were caught. That episode would have been a very serious offence if discovered.

At the beginning, the order from the Germans was "leave everything" – so he did! Having a large barn, he and his father retrieved cars which they had covered and hidden under hay all through the Occupation and were not found by the Germans!

You can rest assured that he still enjoys the area and his surroundings that he has loved all his life, and he is still living in his well-fortified home quietly contented, but very sadly on his own without his beloved Adele who passed away in 1982. I am pleased to say Renaut recently celebrated his 100th birthday with his family.

Adele's Identification Card which everyone had to carry at all times.

Rationing 1944: Food and Heating

Not for the right reasons but 1944 was certainly a year to remember and many thought at long last, after D Day, that the Island would soon be free. The grown-ups were getting impatient that for four years, many had endured real hardship, especially boredom but mainly the loss of freedom and laws which always had to be obeyed! Most days, it was a constant struggle to feed, especially families and the elderly folk who were missing out because they just had to rely purely on rations, which changed from week to week. If one had money to spare, one could perhaps know someone selling on the black market or attend a legal auction sale. With food and commodities having stopped coming from France, everyone would have been grateful for anything at this time and no grumbles about the maggots and very smelly cheese that we had at times on ration.

September 1944 A legal auction sale took place and considering weekly wages were between £2 and £3, you might be interested in the bidding.

1 bottle of sauce	£5 10s
Nutmegs	12d each
Packet of matches	£1 13s
Small tin of Brasso	13 shillings (20 shillings to the pound)
6d tin of Vim	16 shillings
1 bottle baby teat	£3 1s
1 jar of Vaseline	£1
¼pound of tea	£8

November 5th 1944 A letter was written to the International Red Cross at Geneva from Victor Carey, Guernsey's Bailiff, stating: Conditions rapidly deteriorating here. Will soon become impossible. We urge immediate visit of Red Cross representative. All rations drastically reduced.

He gave this list:

Bread finishes 15 December

Sugar finishes 6 January

Soaps and other cleansers – stocks completely exhausted.

Vegetables generally inadequate to supply civilian population through winter.

German consumption heavy.

Salt stocks exhausted.

Clothing and footwear almost exhausted.

Fuel – gas and electricity finish end of year.

Coal stocks exhausted – wood fuel inadequate.

Many essential medical supplies already finished.

Rationing for Christmas 1944

Meat ration for a month 3oz per head

Potatoes 3 lbs a week

It was a very cold winter and people tried burning anything that would burn to keep warm, including broccoli stumps, cowpats, twigs, and old furniture. Germans took what they could find from houses too. Even tar would be mixed with other substances and burnt. It was rationed to a gallon per household, per month.

An order from the military Kommandant was a reduction in bread rationing. From February 5th the week's ration was: infants 1lb, children and invalids 1 ½lbs, and all others 2 lbs until the bread ration eventually ceased on 14 February but as Marjorie Bird wrote in her book, it was an unpleasant musty taste. It tasted sour and very heavy. Not surprising when string, bits of sacking, and even brick dust was found in the loaves, which were frequently mouldy, maggoty and rancid. Biscuits were issued sometimes in place of bread, but they were as hard as ceramic tiles and they had to be soaked in gravy or water for hours at a time before they could be eaten!

Boats laid up

The small local fishing boats were only allowed out at special times or not at all. They had to have a permit to do so. A German escort guard was always in the boat to ensure they kept to the area allowed. Many of the fishermen spoke "patois" which of course was not understood by the Germans. With most of the quota taken by the forces, the fish queue at the market was a very long wait, even with ration books. Especially at the weekends, sometimes 5 hours waiting because the old Guernsey tradition was to eat crab for tea on Sundays. Mum would queue with us, and I have often thought since, how did she manage to cope and keep so cheerful throughout.

From an islander's diary:

Entire ration for 1 week February 1945

1½ oz macaroni

1 oz oatmeal

5 lbs potatoes

⅓ pint separated milk

No butter or cooking fat

No meat, no bread, no salt.

These rations would represent only about 624 calories a day.

February 14th

No bread. Milk reduced to ¼ pint skimmed daily. No butter this week and none for children under 14. No groceries, no meat whatsoever.

24th February

No electricity. No coal. No candles.

27th February weekly ration

1½oz each of flour and macaroni only.

The weekly bill was 2½d (I remember my mother telling me this). Apparently, some-one had groceries delivered through the letter box!

1st March

Last legs of potato and root ration. States 'stew' finished.

8th March

White bread. Thankfully, the Red Cross ship 'Vega' saved many.

25th March

Food scarce. Potatoes and root vegetables finished. New bread 5 lbs per week but not enough. Had to wait a month for potatoes, there was only a few broccoli, cabbage, early lettuce and radishes. With no root vegetables available at all, stinging nettles were cooked as spinach and used for constipation as there was no roughage in the parcels.

With no salt available, a neighbour of ours, Miss May de Garis at number 22, was selling sea water in jars from her home at 2d a jar and that at Le Foulon Road, the States sold sea water every Saturday at 2d a pint as the picture shows. A friend of mine at school, Brenda, who was the eldest of five children, would cycle from the Kings Mills every Saturday to buy sea water at the Rohais, and then cycle for the bread ration from the baker, Mr Jenet at Four Cabot, St Andréws, who rewarded her sometimes with a crust to chew on her way home. It was easier for my mother and I as we would walk down with our pram to Salerie Corner when the tide was in and collect a bucket full, standing and taking care not to fall into the sea from on the steps. Not so lucky, Miss De Garis fell in 6 feet of sea water and had been taken to the Town Hospital suffering from shock.

Our old faithful, the pram, was a blessing again and also when we had to take our "bean jar" with no beans in(!) down to the bake house to cook, mostly

The Saturday queue for sea water at le Rohais

vegetables, if lucky, but I remember the cooking of our cabbage and the smell which was not pleasant (you can imagine when cabbage is simmering for many hours). Many had to queue to take to the bake house and collect as the cooking was overnight and a small charge made, but eventually the demand was so great, the service had to stop. Gas finished completely on December 21st 1944, and was not restored until January 15th 1945.

With no electricity or gas available for cooking and the bake houses ceased, I remember mum somehow heating up food and once hot, she would place it in the centre of sawdust in the large biscuit tin (most people used a hay box at the time) for three or four hours for food to cook. Mrs Dorothy Higgs was the official "Press" cookery expert and food reporter and she gave recipes and food hints on the daily newspaper helping housewives to cope. Her diary of "Life in Guernsey under the Nazis" reminded me of my mother's recipe, especially I wrote in 1985 in "A Child's War", having potato peelings. Mum would always add them to soup and even when having the Red Cross parcels, she would make a sweet of them, cooked with either jam or butter on top. Bread supposedly would finish on 15 December but it did last a little longer until 14 February but what we ate then was a mystery!

Working at the flour mills in La Charroterie, a baker told me that the flour was like cement, "awful stuff, old and grey and given to us locals as pudding flour". The men had to crush the German flour with a crusher.

The baker's flour was given on ration too but Mrs Higgs mentioned the flour was of unknown origin and when sifted, more than half of the bulk remained on the sieve and appeared to be chopped straw and sawdust. I remember well seeing the maggots in bread and cheese and having many husks in our 'porridge' which we had to spit out all the time.

Unfortunately, none of the flour was sifted during the latter stage and all this was worrying Mr Rex Bragg who was the main distributor of flour to bakeries around the island. His business was near us on the Esplanade. The family knew Mr Bragg well and in talking to him, he once told me that it was a good thing we did not know of the contents. He was a Christian and a sincere sensitive man, and it concerned him a great deal, but he had no choice but to distribute it. Now he has passed away, one can hear his recording of these times at the archives of the Imperial War Museum in London. Mr Bragg did not want the recording available for public knowledge before he died. Mr Bragg like everyone on the island must have been so thankful to have good wholesome bread again on March the 8th, it was wonderful and many prayers were answered that day.

Above: The long awaited flour arrives and is taken to Braggs on the Esplanade; St John's personnel and Germans in attendance.

The Red Cross Saved Lives

From June 1944, our food naturally stopped coming from France. The British and other forces had landed and the grown-ups had high hopes of at last, Liberation! But it was not to be for almost another year. During November, there was talk and rumours all over the island that at the end of the month, a ship was in Jersey and would be in Guernsey on 28 November. We children at school, were excited of course and we were given the day off to see the boat come in. Disappointment for everyone as still no boat or parcels. Rumours were still rife, everyone wanted news but apparently, the boat was unavoidably delayed and still no boat for Christmas or Boxing Day. During this time, food and all commodities were extremely short. Rationing at the end of February 1945 was issued and for the two weeks into March, was five pounds of potatoes, two ounces of flour and that was it! No gas, no electricity, no coal available for a year and no wood for fires, cooking or anything. A notice appeared in the press that there was only water available for drinking and cooking and none could be used for washing clothes, flushing toilets or even washing ourselves. Difficult to imagine these times and one can fully understand our excitement and parents everywhere when looking forward to wonderful food parcels that were promised to come during the winter of 1945.

It was not until late in 1944 that a Red Cross message at last was received in Geneva. Every day hopes were high but it was not until Wednesday 27th December 1944 – at long last, the dramatic news came that the Vega was sighted from Pleinmont. This news certainly went around the Island very quickly and the boat could not come into Guernsey quick enough. Everyone had waited so long because the majority of Islanders were very hungry, many starving and so looking forward to a good wholesome meal and to think at last, the boat was almost here. No wonder there was excitement to be felt with everyone you spoke to. Food that really a lot of us could not remember but knew it would do us good and just longed to know what was coming in the parcels.

The Vega

The Red Cross ship was nearing at last, but there was trouble when berthing her. The Germans would on no condition allow the Vega to be berthed where the Guernsey Harbour Master told them where to berth. Being an old ship, he said she should NOT go near the Fruit Export sheds on the Careening Hard as the bottom of the harbour was not flat and she would be damaged at low tide. It was a case of there or not at all, and the representative from Geneva, Switzerland had no say in the matter. It berthed there and hence the keel was damaged. The ship was subsequently repaired in Portugal and her next visit to Guernsey was therefore delayed.

On 27 December, during early evening, our family joined a crowd on the sea front pavement as near as we could get to the harbour and at last, she came in slowly into the harbour and everyone began to cheer loudly – all St Peter Port could hear the cheers as thousands of Islanders were on the Esplanade to witness the arrival of food. Many prayers were answered that evening, many were so thankful and I am sure shed silent tears, I know Mum and I did.

Bill Green wrote his thoughts in his book "Guernsey Green". The Vega turned towards the London berth where she tied up. Suddenly, cheering broke out from the thousands of joyful Islanders who wanted to witness and be part of that historic moment. Ask any Guernseyman who was in the Island during the Occupation, where they were when the Vega arrived with its precious cargo of Red Cross parcels and they will tell you precisely".

The Canadian and New Zealand parcels were taken from the ship by the German railway from the White Rock to St George's Hall. They were then distributed by horse and cart to the shops for collection by the St John's organisation. There was great excitement everywhere when we were issued with the parcels on 31 December and the food tasted delicious. Details of food in my book "A Time for Memories".

It was just wonderful collecting our parcels and seeing especially chocolate. We had almost forgotten the taste of it, but loved both the Canadian and New Zealand chocolate, and would compare the size and taste of which one we preferred at school the next day. Strangely enough what I remember most is the excitement of having bread after being without for so long and all the family were so grateful and excited on that first day of that special loaf.

Some friends I have spoken to in the past, felt that when the wonderful food parcels arrived, with such relief, it was better than Liberation Day. I can only imagine how thankful the grown-ups were as so many more would have died of starvation without them.

Left: Elizabeth Lihou at The National Trust Shop with an original Red Cross parcel.

Every visit meant a great deal to us and always warmly welcomed by crowds of Islanders. The second visit was on 7th February 1945, with cod liver oil and malt brought especially for us children who were found to have lost weight, after having no bread for three weeks. But at last, on the third visit, 500 tons of beautiful white flour came which was 'manitoba' flour from the finest quality wheat. There were six visits in all and on the final visit, the Canadian parcels contained flour, sugar, yeast, biscuits (lovely for breakfast), clothing, footwear, household and toilet soaps, salt, diesel oil and medical supplies. A gift of honey was also sent from her Royal Highness Princess Elizabeth for every child on the island. Having had no bread for three weeks, it was just like having cake, and we ate it as it was – no need for anything to flavour it. We shall never forget the taste of a wonderful large round white loaf which we bought from the bakery. Incidentally, the Germans checked flour sacks to make sure no ammunitions were hidden inside but they did not interfere with nor take any of the parcels despite being very hungry themselves. The Islanders appreciated so much what the Red Cross had done for us with letters to and fro from 1941 and to the food parcels in 1945 and ever since, the Red Cross charity has a special place in our hearts. The "Vega" was finally broken up in Stockholm in 1954. We shall always be grateful for her visits. By May 18th, the total amount given to the Duke of Gloucester's Red Cross and St John's Fund, amounting to £42,071 and 12 shillings, 4 pence. (More of the Red Cross written in a Time for Memories).

You will see the letter I wrote on March 5th 1945 to a dear friend, Mrs Grace Mahy, who gave me this letter before she died. All through the Occupation her husband, Sid Mahy, worked at the Harbour and managed very occasionally to bring a little treat home. They both had no children of their own and must have been fond of Joyce and I as they would share and make a special effort to give us a nice tea after school as often as they could.

These acts of kindness were typical of everyone during the Occupation as Mr and Mrs Mahy were strangers to us until they made themselves known when they first saw us dancing on the stage.

There was also another young person, a George Le Page, who made friends. He lived in the country at St Andrews and would come all the way by his horse and cart to bring milk and a few vegetables whenever he could from his farm. To us 'townies' it was also a treat to have a ride with George in his

30 Carrichonn
1 St Peter Port.
local.
5th March.

Dear Mrs Mahy,

I am very sorry to hear you have been ill this last fortnight. It was very funny but last night in bed, I was thinking of you, and I made up my mind to write to you. When Joyce came home on Saturday when she said that you weren't there, I thought it was queer, but never thought of you being bad. Well, changing the subject, What do you think of the pancakes? Aren't they lovely, as soon as they arrived, mummy opened the butter, chocolate and the porridge

Joyce and I had this morning, and what delicious cocoa. We had 2 parcels with oatmeal and cocoa but none with 2 sugars. We are looking out for the "Vega" they say that was off Pleinmont Point this afternoon. But you hear so many rumours, we don't know what to believe. (On Friday we had 2 lb of Cod liver oil and Malt (all school children) which come by the Vega last time. Aren't it lovely.

Well, cheerio for now, cheer up as the news in good and we shall soon have bread. What's that? I shall come to see you to-morrow about 3 P.m or just after.

With lots of love.
From Molly.
x x x x x x
x x x x x x
x x x

Hoping that the boat will be in.

135

Left and top: Collecting Red Cross
parcels from the High Street

old horse and cart. (I should add, Mother kept well out of the way, as she was very nervous of all horses. Many times on our country trips, we had to go into gardens to avoid horses because of how she felt.)

Mum did appreciate a great kindness from a Mr Hubert who had a stall in the market. He asked me one day if my mother could go and see him. He asked if we

✚ PMC

R.C.B. GUERNSEY.

Deutsches Rotes Kreuz

Präsidium / Auslandsdienst
Berlin SW 61, Blücherplatz 2

A   43995

ANTRAG

an die *Agence Centrale des Prisonniers de Guerre, Genf*
— Internationales Komitee vom Roten Kreuz —
auf Nachrichtenvermittlung

REQUÊTE

*de la Croix-Rouge Allemande, Présidence, Service Étranger
à l'Agence Centrale des Prisonniers de Guerre, Genève
— Comité International de la Croix-Rouge —
concernant la correspondance*

1. Absender
   Expéditeur

   Mrs. N. Woodland. Falkland. L'Islet.

   ST. SAMPSONS. GUERNSEY. C.I.

   bittet, an
   prie de bien vouloir faire parvenir à

   sister.

2. Empfänger
   Destinataire

   Mrs. E. Palmer. C/o R.C.B. 751. Gaddum
   House. Queen Street. MANCHESTER.
   ENGLAND.

   folgendes zu übermitteln / *ce qui suit :*

   (Höchstzahl 25 Worte !)
   (*25 mots au plus !*)

   Dear Edith. Everythiig well. Joan

   living at Amballes, Ley happy at

   Bungalow. Lovely having Margaret

   with you. Malcolm very good, average

   school. Love all. Nora.

   (Datum / *Date*)

3. Empfänger antwortet umseitig 21.4.43
   Destinataire répond au verso

   (Unterschrift / *Signature*)

   (Mrs) N. Woodland.

would accept some vegetables most weekends as a gift, if we could collect them. He was always a little tearful when seeing me because I reminded him so much of his daughter, Noella, who had evacuated. When she returned after the Occupation we made friends and yes, we were very much alike and of the same age. What a blessing for my family, and I hope the sad separation was helped a little by helping us and by our gratitude.

I have mentioned the Red Cross letters that would take months to send and receive back in Guernsey and only five words at the beginning were allowed to be sent. Later one was allowed 25 words. The Germans censored them all, but occasionally coded ones did get through and were overlooked such as one sent to friends in Guernsey by a headmaster who had been evacuated with his pupils. The message read 'All children very fit. Tommy, Joe and Sam's boys working hard. Doing very good work. Should graduate with honours in near future.' This caused some delight when it was printed in the local paper. The names represented countries of course: Tommy: Britain, Russia: Joe and Sam was America.

Another example here is shown (on page 137) and Malcolm Woodland explains. His aunt, a widow, Mrs Palmer, owned a property in Les Amballes. Her daughter Margaret had evacuated with her school and Mrs Palmer got away later on the last Dorey's coal boat from St. Sampson's harbour. Joan had also been evacuated so when reading the message she knew this couldn't be so. In the message, she rightly guessed who it was, the Germans were living in her house. As Malcolm says, it didn't need a code-breaker to work that out! He also has the original Red Cross letter.

The message suggests that Malcolm was very good at school and I have appreciated his vivid memories that have helped in writing this book. He and his wife are particularly proud of their granddaughter Amy who entered this Occupation poem in the 2010 Eisteddfod of music, dance and speech. It is pleasing to know and important that Guernsey's future generations discover the island's history, and the meaning of being occupied.

Occupied now
Curfew at night
Controls on activities
Under the Germans
People are scared
Air raid warning sound
Times are hard
I miss my dada
Operation Overlord
Now we are free

Amy Woodland – age 10. 2010

Adjudicator's remarks: Honours Certificate. This is an extraordinarily good poem. A wonderfully poignant picture of Occupation life. You are an exceptionally talented writer Amy.

White Rock, St Peter Port harbour, Red Cross parcels being loaded on the railway to be transported to St George's Hall.

Hungry German Soldiers At Our Dustbins

There was a great deal of stealing by the Germans after we received our Red Cross parcels. Many homes were entered and food was stolen, also fields and gardens where there might be vegetables or anything edible. We saw the Germans looking in our dustbins and taking empty tins out, checking to see if anything, however small, was left. This was a worrying time for farmers as so many of their cows were milked during the night. Nothing was safe and livestock was frequently taken during the last 11 months. The majority of German troops stole during 1944 even from German stores and 2,900 cases of stealing goods from German stores were recorded.

There was a soldier who came into a bakery and held a 1 kilo loaf which had to last him 5 days. It contained oat flour which in his opinion was uneatable. He was going to collect stinging nettles for soup and was buying carrageen moss.

A couple were shot dead in their St Peter Port home, for their food parcel.

Another incident was reported to the German Commandant in St Martins. A German lady who was married to a Guernsey man and had lived on the island for many years, reported that Germans on horse-back were trampling fields where crops of vegetables were planted and jumping over hedges like in races. This was serious to them and very much annoyed them. Early one morning again in St Martins, a farmer's wife saw a German soldier cutting a broccoli and leaving the leaves in the field. She called her husband, who at once got his hay fork and told the German to go. The German had an army pistol in his belt, and fired at the farmer who died instantly in front of his wife. He was 35 years old, and the German said he acted in self-defence, so nothing came of it. (The Guernseyman of course had no gun at the time).

The Germans brought over a thousand lovely horses, but there were only 600 left after Liberation. These were later sold to Guernsey farmers. The Germans were certainly hungry and many cats and dogs went missing at this time, and their horses were eaten. The 'Lost' column in the Press contained many pleas for lost pets.

Stealing was rife, although one had to wait in turn to serve your sentence. 14 days hard labour was given to a man who stole a small bunch of rhubarb. Two greenhouses workers were sentenced to 6 months hard labour for stealing milk. If found hoarding food (more than a month's ration of food), one would be imprisoned (this was a law throughout the five years).

Even towards the end of the Occupation, prison sentences were still handed out to the islanders, but many were released because of so little food. One man illegally slaughtered a cow and heifer. He was sentenced to a year's hard labour and fined £300. I hope he was released early enough to enjoy the meat!

Farmers and owners of animals could at times fool the Germans, but all livestock had to be registered and kept under strict control. There were always ways and means of hiding animals and keeping Germans at bay. Many times animals were taken indoors overnight, especially rabbits. Friendly neighbours often helped out too. I've heard of a pig being hidden in a pram during a search!

The Germans we used to see frequently passing along Les Canichers were getting thinner and thinner by the day, their uniforms were just hanging off them. "Otto", the Nazi, was among these. I doubt very much if he could have run or kicked very hard at this time. Formerly, he had been such a well and heavy built man with very big shoulders and features, now his body was bent over and very frail. As a whole too, the Germans were very despondent and low in spirit as the war was now swinging against them. When we were first occupied, and for a good while after, it seemed they were always marching in groups and singing in the streets of the town. Now, all was quiet, no more shouting, no more singing their familiar song "I.E.I.O!"

Liberation

8 May 1945 I took this photograph in Les Canichers of family, friends and neighbours after hearing Winston Churchill's broadcast: "Our dear Channel Islands will be free today". My mother is centre front with a rosette, Dad at the back with a flag, and Grandpa on the far front left.

Now every day was one less to tolerate under the German rule. Rumours were still going round as they had been all through the years, but after waiting and praying for so long, our 'day' was soon to come. The heading on the front page of the 'Guernsey Press' told us we could 'fly our Flags' at 3pm May 8th. At last, what excitement and relief to Mum, Dad and everyone. Upstairs, Mum told us to get the flags out, ready to fly them across the street. With a radio getting an airing at long last, neighbours and the family got together in the street to listen to our dear Winston Churchill giving his famous speech. We did not worry if Germans were around us or whether they were passing by, they took no notice, the radio was in an upstairs bedroom window on the ledge, and we were all gathered together in the road. I remember him loud and clear, "Our dear Channel Islands will be free". I took the "Liberation" photograph with an old box camera Mum and Dad had not handed in and can only assume there was a film inside from all those years before.

May 9th 1945 was to be our day. I don't think anyone could really sleep well that previous night, we all had so much to look forward to. I remember Joyce and I wakening early around 6am, our first thought was to look out of the window. We soon woke the household as clearly we could see the ships in the distance moored in front of Herm. My mother, sister and I soon got dressed and dashed off down towards the harbour. At the Weighbridge islanders were gathering, but seeing we were down early, we were just behind the barbed wire gates and the constables and a German guard who were to keep us off the harbour. The harbour being out of bounds and heavily mined! Our eyes were glued to the road as we could not see if the boats had come into the harbour. We all wanted that first glimpse of British soldiers. By this time an hour seemed ages, but we all waited patiently until that smart party coming up the Harbour got bigger and closer and we just could not hold back our excitement any longer, and when someone opened the barbed wire gate, we made a dash towards them.

The advance party of Operation Nestegg, known as the Omelette Party, seen here outside the States Offices, North Esplanade. The first soldiers ashore, with Nobby Hamon. *(CIOS)*

Liberation group – what a wonderful picture, May 9th.

I was there! Early morning at the Weighbridge.

They looked wonderfully smart with bayonets held high - we all ran as fast as we could and I was amongst the first people to greet them. We were hugging them, kissing them, laughing and crying at the same time. Even the soldiers were overcome and I am sure they had never seen or felt anything like it before. I have received letters since, telling me how emotional they also felt. Everyone was overwhelmed with relief. The soldiers had their hats and bayonets flying in all directions, it was a wonderful moment and if I live to be 100, I shall never forget it. All day, May 9th 1945, was a wonderful day! We loved and hugged so many people. Everyone was on top of the world.

There was so much cheering and love for those 22 boys. When, at last they reorganised and collected their helmets and rifles etc and were ready to march again, we followed them along the sea front to the States office and then to the Royal Court House steps, where the ceremony of raising the Union Jack took place.

It was while still on the Esplanade and very soon the bells of the Town

Church rang out. They sounded wonderful after the five years of silence. There were British planes coming and going overhead flying quite low and those sounded wonderful too. A Pathé film unit set up loud speakers for everyone to hear messages from the family and folk on the mainland sending their love and thoughts of coming home soon. The film unit also made the Liberation film which although short, it is a wonderful reminder for us who were there. So much to enjoy and excitement for us all. However, it was the singing of "Sarnia Cherie" that was so emotional for us all – and is still when we hear our national song.

I seemed to want to be in several places at the same time, there was so much excitement going on, but it was the case of following the crowds most of the time as all the streets were packed in the town. I remember very well I ate only a couple of biscuits all through the day and these were given to me

Left: Tank Landing craft 516 in the Old Harbour 14 May 1945. Above: An amphibious GMC truck DUKW known as a Duck arrives on the slipway of the Old Harbour 14 May 1945. *(CIOS)*

by a soldier; a sailor also gave me an orange! I just flung my arms around him when I thanked him, I was so thrilled. Mind you, I hadn't a clue to what it tasted like or how I was going to tackle it!

Although our home was only five minutes' walk away from the town, it never occurred to me to go home at all during the day. My father was also lost in the crowd and in the excitement. All Guernsey must have been out and there were tears, singing and laughter everywhere. It is difficult for me to put into words the happiness I felt, as young as I was, I felt such deep gratitude.

60th anniversary of Liberation Day, 9 May 2005. Me in a wagon wearing my Guernsey bonnet.

I never dreamt I could feel such happiness and exhilaration.

All through the 5 years, the people on the island had felt very close having to cope with hunger, boredom and frustration, they shared everyone's troubles and tried to help each other, now it was time to rejoice and be happy. All the Forces that landed were wonderful too, sharing in 'our day'; we had no cares that day, just thankfulness and love for our British who at last had come, and many more of the Force 135 were to arrive during that afternoon and the following days.

We were all very excited when we eventually arrived home and just did not want 9th May to end, but of course we had everything good to look forward to. My mother incidentally, had cheered and sang so much that she lost her voice completely for a few days, and for months and months had a strained and croaky voice! Even up and into her 80s, she always said it was all worthwhile as in all her life she had never known a day like it before or since! My father was also happy when we arrived home as the soldier leading the small group was an old friend of his, Sergeant Nobby Hamon who with Dad, was a football referee before the war.

When Force 135 landed, there were many thousands of Germans still on the island, and armed, but there was no resistance from them.

I am pleased to say not one of our family saw another German soldier on this day or afterwards, not even Otto. Maybe just as well, but my father had long forgotten his words in the 'heated moment' and now for Guernsey, and for him, everything was looking 'prima'.

Many of us were surprised and tickled when we stood at the Old Harbour (now the Victoria Marina) on Saturday May 12th. We saw the large American ship arrive and open the large doors at the back. Then we watched all different vehicles drive off and pass us up to the slipway. Many of the lorries, jeeps and motorbikes had the names of their sweethearts or wives painted on them and the Americans were throwing packets of cigarettes, soap, sweets etcetera, adding to the excitement to us all. Apparently iron netting had been laid and at low tide, this ship could enter, but then we never expected to see a very tall gentleman with bowler hat, an umbrella and attaché case, walk from the ship smartly dressed entirely in black. Many cheers and smiles went up from us – we standing there plainly dressed, so it amused everyone. We eventually knew he was Mr C.D. Bickmore, a civil servant, and he was carrying important plans for the complete rehabilitation of the island. It was a strange sight I'll always remember and with many others, we sang 'They'll always be an England' with tears, cheers and laughter, then and for many days to come.

To sum up our Liberation day and feelings, these last words must come from my mother who sent this message dated 11th May 1945 to dear friends Edie and Billy Wilcox living at the time in Yorkshire. Luckily and thankfully they had decided to evacuate back to England in 1940 (as they were English born) and we had received little news from them during the 5 years of the Occupation.

Our dear Aunty Edie had saved this very first message from the family until she died nearly forty years later.

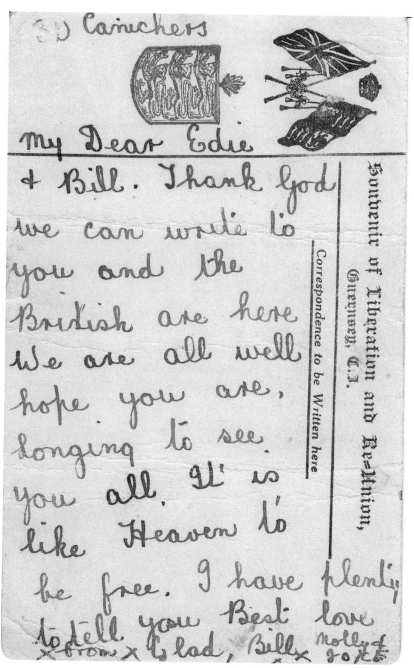

39 Canichers

my Dear Edie
+ Bill. Thank God
we can write to
you and the
British are here
We are all well
hope you are,
longing to see.
you all. It is
like Heaven to
be free. I have plenty
to tell you Best love
x from x Glad, Billy x nolly &
go x

Mum's letter to Aunty Edie

Freddie Frinton came for Tea

"My mother's cheerful and friendly disposition soon brought in many of the 'Liberation boys' and we had many a happy evening with plenty of tales to tell and a sing-song around the piano. The majority of these boys were Welsh and had wonderful voices. Amongst the friends was Freddie Frinton who came over to entertain the troops in "Stars in Battledress" and will be remembered later as a comedian on the television in a series with Thora Hird. It was whilst Joyce and I were playing ball in the Canichers that he joined in and was welcomed in home like the many others. I remember well us walking with him to show off 'Les Vauxbelets Chapel' and drinking milk (him also) straight from the cow when offered some by a farmer. I think we all looked upon these men as 'Super Men' and we admired them all. We kept in touch with Freddie until he died and still write to family of two other Liberation boys who were living in South Wales. Many of the liberation soldiers have since returned to the island over the years, as they had many happy memories and wanted to meet up with the friends they made.

Guernsey has celebrated Liberation Day on 9 May every year since 1945, and it is an official holiday, and hopefully it will always remain so. At the 50th anniversary of the Liberation in 1995, to show our appreciation, all Force 135 veterans and their families were invited to the island, to share our big day with us. HRH Prince Charles also joined the celebrations, and what a wonderful time everyone had, especially so the Liberation veterans who all received a special medal from the States of Guernsey.

I received letters from many members of the Liberation Forces in 1995 (50th anniversary of the Liberation). The letters spoke of how they were full of emotion when so many islanders showed such gratitude to them when they arrived on that first Liberation Day 50 years ago. They admitted being tearful and had never forgotten the arrival they received. I have chosen a few sentences and lines from some of those letters.

Ernest Bevins "Bev" writes: When we finally landed it was kisses and hugs from the ladies, the men shook hands, patted our backs and asked if we had any cigs. We gave the children sweets, and they thought it was Christmas. The Germans had used slave labourers over there. Many died and the Russian prisoners we had to de-louse and feed them. Then they were sent to the mainland for hospitalisation. They looked like pictures of people from the concentration camps, and their staring eyes said "thank you". The Germans were all imprisoned and made to work clearing the island of mines etc. They had still left some booby traps for us.

One thing sticks in my mind. I was standing by my lorry, the lads were clearing out a jerry store, making sure there were no booby traps, when an old lady came to me (it was lovely weather), with tears in her eyes and she said "There you are! I said an English soldier would have the first strawberry and you're it!" And I had to stand there and eat it, and I cried with her.

Mr J Clydesdale wrote on 25 January 1995: I remember coming ashore in the evening sunshine and in a street near the harbour, a lady invited us into her house for a drink of water. It was probably all she had in the house, she just wanted to say "Hello" and we shared her happiness.

Stan Crowther from Rotherham wrote: I am sure none of us felt at all like heroes (we islanders thought they were!), the heroes were local people like, for example, a chap called George (I forget his second name) who had been an amateur radio enthusiast before the Occupation, and risked deportation by building crystal sets on which his friends listened to the BBC – but it was good to be involved in the Liberation of the only bit of the British Islands occupied by the enemy.

Mrs Fay Payne wrote of her husband George who had passed away in 1994, but surely would have had an interesting story to relate of May 9th 1945 as Mrs Payne wrote: George loved Guernsey. He was a survivor of HMS Charybdis which had been sunk in the Channel, and some of his ship-mates were washed ashore and buried in Guernsey. Every year we used to come to the commemorative service for the survivors. My husband George was also on the "Bulldog" and was in Guernsey in 1945 when the Germans came aboard to sign the surrender of the Channel Islands. All these events made him feel very close to your island.

Sydney Searalt of Cumbria wrote: Whilst I'm sure no-one in this country at the time thought you were having a picnic, I don't think anyone really appreciated the extent of your hardships, the deprivation and the lack of freedom you endured, all of which you have faithfully recorded in your books. It really is amazing how everyone coped in such circumstances, but when put to the test, there seems no limit to human endurance.

More letters can be found in the book "A Time for Memories", and there is much more about the Liberation and afterwards in "Reflections of Guernsey".

Molly and Liberation Soldier at Woodcote in 1995
at home with medal showing

After Liberation & Force 135

For many weeks after the excitement of Liberation, our home was always filled with happy times enjoying the Liberation 'Boys' of Force 135 and neighbours and friends. We could see from our home the mail boats come into the harbour, with the returning evacuees. We went off to see hundreds arrive with friends and relations to greet them – scenes of emotion and happiness when at last they were home after more than five years to their loved ones. Mum and dad knew so many who returned. It was not easy for children at first to recognise especially their fathers and I have spoken to some of my age who had settled very well with their UK families and who really wanted to stay, although the majority could not get home quick enough.

I have listened to André's tape of his years in Wolverhampton and when talking of his homecoming into our harbour, the tape went quiet for many minutes – he too was overcome and could not speak and this recording was made in the 1980's for the London War Museum archives. The joy, relief and memories were still clear to him. I shall never forget when I was visiting my aunt, dad's sister Mrs Win Salmon and my grandmother, dad's mum (Mrs Brassell), who also stayed on the Island and whom I have written about in my two subsequent books and saw my uncle, dad's brother, arrive for the first time, visiting in his lovely smart blue air force uniform. We had been so used to drab smelly, grey/green and scruffy uniforms for so long, I could not help crying and was really sobbing in his arms. The uniform and Uncle Mick must have meant so much to me and it meant freedom, seeing him and others again.

The Liberation soldiers left Guernsey in Autumn 1945. Middle row, Molly (first left), Mother, Joyce (Sister) Aunt, Uncle and Cousins at the harbour.

Letter of Pride

After the celebration of Liberation Day had died down a little, my father suggested I should write to the man we felt we owed so much to, Winston Churchill. Every islander felt so thankful he had given us our freedom and we were full of gratitude towards him. I sat down and wrote, little expecting a reply, but was so thrilled when an envelope arrived with the '10 Downing Street', Whitehall and PRIME MINISTER stamped on it. I was so proud and over the page is the write-up in the Guernsey Press printed the next day.

To this day, I have treasured this letter from the man 'Our Hero' at the time to whom the islanders owed so much and to whom we all felt and still feel great affection for now. It was disappointing for us that he was unable to visit the islands after we were liberated but we were all thrilled to see our King George VI and Queen Elizabeth when they both paid a visit on 7 June 1945. We, the schoolchildren, had pride of place and were very excited to see them both, when at Candie Gardens. There was really great rejoicing and excitement for weeks after the war ended when all the families were reunited gradually together again, and the school children returned.

10, Downing Street,
Whitehall.

    I have been deeply
touched by all the messages
of good will which have
reached me at this time.
Thank you so much for your
kind thought.

                 Winston S. Churchill

        May, 1945.

PRIME MINISTER

Sends Message to Guernsey School Girl

Thirteen-year-old Molly Finigan, of 30, Canichers, St. Peter-Port, was the proudest girl in Guernsey yesterday: she received a reply personally signed by Prime Minister Winston Churchill to her message of gratitude at our liberation.

On May 9th Molly sent the following post card Souvenir of Liberation and Re-union to the Right Honourable Winston Churchill: " On behalf of all schoolchildren, including myself, we express our gratitude and thanks for our liberation and freedom after five years of hardship. May God bless you and your loved ones. I remain a faithful admirer.—Molly Finigan (13 years)."

Little did Molly expect a reply. But yesterday back came a message from the Prime Minister, bearing his personal autograph. It read: " I have been deeply touched by all the messages of goodwill which have reached me at this time. Thank you so much for your kind thoughts."

WINSTON S. CHURCHILL.

The Victory Parade, London 1946

After a year of celebrations and of Guernsey getting back to normal, there were special children's film shows etcetera, and there was more excitement when my sister, Joyce, was chosen to go to London and would be amongst others to represent Guernsey and the Channel Islands in the Victory Parade. It was to take place during May 1946 and the group would be from Guernsey, Jersey and Sark. Not Alderney as it had been more or less fully evacuated so no-one represented the northern Island. I can remember the excitement at home and I am sure all the children were the same, just waiting for the big day.

Mr Frank Stroobant was also invited and he describes in his interesting book "One Man's War" what conditions were like there. He wrote that the morning began with a short flight to Jersey and then they were transferred to a larger plane. Frank said it was a York aircraft of the Kings Flight. Apparently, Guernsey's runway was not long enough for this plane to take off, but I am sure this all added to everyone's excitement.

He wrote of the awful wet weather when waiting for the procession to start from Hyde Park. After a very long wait, the group heard the distant strains of a military band – then they were marshalled by a guards officer and were given allotted places. Frank was very proud to represent and be amongst so many from the great Commonwealth of Nations and to see many thousands of people who lined the route. One thing did sadden him greatly though. That the Channel Islands had no identification at all, had no flag, neither a banner but every group walking had something stating where they came from. He writes "the absence of our party's emblem" was not commented on by the crowd until we halted at the end of Oxford Street, before wheeling right into

Guernsey group in London. Joyce centre 1st right.

Charing Cross Road. Some wise guy from the windows of Frascati's Restaurant shouted "Where do you mugs come from?" Frank had expected a question such as this and shouted back "Wormwood Scrubs!" London. Typical of the Frank Stroobant I knew! After this, Frank said it was loud cheers all the way and much laughter. I am sure the young and old must have felt really honoured to be part of this march and for the children, like my sister Joyce, must have had their eyes opened to see Big Ben, Trafalgar Square, Buckingham Palace, the trains and trams and big shops in London. How different London was compared to little Guernsey, and what a thrill it must have been and to be entertained so well for a week. Frank Stroobant felt it was the honour done to our Island by the recognition of all that it had suffered and stood for the period of history which we sincerely hope will never be repeated.

More about the Liberation and afterwards in "Reflections of Guernsey".

Co-incidences from 1940, 1980 & 2011

André and a school friend, John, arrived with other weary children in Glasgow with the St Joseph's School group. They were taken with teachers to Dixon Hall, Carthwright Road. John and André were not chosen to live with foster parents or anyone after lining up, so they remained with others at the Hall and attended a Catholic Church called 'Our Lady of Lourdes' on Paisley Road until their families found out a few weeks later where they were staying. André was eventually reunited with his family and they spent the war years living in Wolverhampton. What troubled André (and many other children I expect) was understanding the Scottish accent whilst living there but he also found the Wolverhampton was far worse! He returned home at 17 and had worked at an ammunition factory for some 2 years.

Dixon Hall, Glasgow at Evacuation Time
with courtesy of J. Willaims.

Mr Cooper

A young teacher Philip Cooper travelled with the boys to Glasgow and was well loved and respected by the boys and islanders alike throughout his life.

Quite a co-incidence came to light whilst at home in Guernsey some 40 years later. Felix Chaciewitz (from Poland) ran a hotel opposite our guest house with his wife Sylvia. There were many winter evenings when we met together for a friendly chat, and one evening the conversation turned to Scotland. Apparently, in 1940 at the 'Our Lady of Lourdes' Church in Glasgow, there was a special service and André, John and some 18 – 20 Guernsey boys learned a Polish anthem to sing in the church especially for the Polish airmen unit who were stationed nearby and who attended the service. You have probably guessed that, yes! Felix was there in uniform and he remembered very well the boys singing and standing especially for the airmen, as they had a camp close to the church. Singing in Polish, the words of the anthem was 'March! March! Darbrowski, on to win Liberation, with your arm to lead us, we shall save the nation!' This particular evening turned out to be a very special time for André and Felix, quite an evening but emotional too.

Yvonne Fisher

After André died in November 2010, the following season I did not feel like selling books at the market (only once) or sea front (one Sunday), but one day in May, with good weather promised, I decided to telephone Mr Peter de Sausmarez and asked if I could attend at the lovely, weekly Sausmarez Manor famers' market the following day. What a morning it turned out to be with many tears of happiness!

A young lady approached and bought a jar of my home made fig jam and looked at my books and with talking, she told me she was working on the island on a 6 month licence. Because her mother had died last year, she wanted to find out if anyone on the island would remember or know of her grand-dad who she knew had stayed in Guernsey for a short while many years ago. She did not mention his surname but I said the best bet would be to contact the 'Guernsey Press' newspaper, and also maybe go to the very helpful staff at the Priaulx Library. Before she left, photographs were mentioned and she said she might go to her home and bring back photographs she had of her grandfather who also had since died.

She did return and showed me a smart young man (guessing in his early 20s), and as soon as I saw him, I said he looked like a very young Pat Sullivan. Immediately, Yvonne (Fisher) said "that's his name!" Well, it seemed unbelievable as she hadn't asked anyone else and I knew this young lady's grandfather,

Young Pat Sullivan *with courtesy of Yvonne Fisher*

especially when she showed me an older Pat Sullivan in uniform. He was one of the friendly Liberation soldiers of Force 135 who would come into our home and made to feel so welcome as we felt so much gratitude towards the British who gave us back our freedom.

The surprise and shock of finding out this news brought us together with much hugging and many tears, and it was just wonderful for Yvonne, especially when a third photograph was shown with me sitting at Vazon beach with her smiling mother as a young girl (I remembered her too), and her grand-mother and grand-dad to the left of me in the photo, plus my father (with cap) and my uncle (front). My mother would probably have been helping at the Café at the 'Peary Nook' across the road as she always did, almost daily. Another photograph which must have been given by her grandfather was one of my mother and father in Rose Villa's garden (our home), with handwriting saying "Glad and Bill Finigan at Beryl's wedding" (my cousin, see page 170).

The family had been invited over for a holiday at 'Rose Villa' like so many others and returned for holidays when they went back after service. I'm so pleased I was there to help and to remember one of the many who were friends and who joined us during the very happy times after May 9th 1945. I think this must be proof of what these men meant to us islanders as, without hesitation, to know her grandfather's name (with others) after some 69 years, and the generosity of my parents to them and other families. Yvonne was also surprised and pleased to see her grandfather's photograph, taken in

The Family with the Sullivan's at Vazon Beach *with courtesy of Yvonne Fisher*

1945, with other Liberation servicemen of Force 135 in my book "A Time for Memories".

Yvonne did continue working on the island longer and enjoyed very much joining me on two Liberation Days, selling and talking to everyone. Sadly, she left the island after May 9th this year (2013) but she intends to come back and to keep in touch, which she has come back to help me just for the day in 2014 and hopefully will come back for the big 70th anniversary next year.

With dad driving the family, Liberation 'Boys' and their wives & sons on a picnic. Early 1950's. HAPPY TIMES!

Letters from Germany

During late June 2011, I received a very nice 'thank you' letter. It was from Regina Krauer in Germany, who said she appreciated the lack of hatred in my book, towards her forefathers and their actions for which she was 'truly ashamed'. She wanted to express her great respect for myself, my family and all the brave inhabitants of Guernsey. It was a pleasure answering her very nice letter. Then I received a special Christmas surprise from her and her students at their university in Zerbst (Francisceum), just in time for me to write back and thank all of them personally before the Christmas break.

Being a teacher of English, Regina Krauer explained she chose two girls to take part, 'to be me' and to imagine I had come to the school and 'I' was asked many questions about the Occupation and my time in school. Each of the 17 students wrote letters to me, about what they felt they had learned from 'me'. The letters certainly made interesting reading. There were ten photographs of the students in class, and three photographs of the groups listening to Frau Krauer and the research about England and the Channel Islands during World War II.

What a lovely parcel to receive and I was really quite touched by these young people. Whilst there were many comments from the students, Max Blume wrote "I have never seen such a cool old woman with an awful past like this!" I would like to have met him and the other writers.

Also enclosed was a very nice pencil drawing on an A2 sheet. The artist, Anna, wrote…

"My picture is divided into three parts. On the left you can see a crying woman. She resembles the desperation people on Guernsey must have endured during World War II. On the right, there is a white dove which symbolises hope and the people's wish for peace. I think people did not live life without hope even if the future did not look too good, as what is the meaning of life when there is no hope for a better future? That is why I assume they did not lose their positive attitude towards the future. In the last part, the centre, you can see roses which stand for a film we have watched. It is about a young girl who lives in Guernsey during the German Occupation. In general, we dealt a lot with that topic and I hope you like the picture. Anna"

I would have loved to have printed all the many letters from them, and also so many over the years that I have received. I treasure them all and especially drawings from children after talking to them at Guernsey schools. It has brought me a lot of pleasure, knowing that children are interested in Guernsey's history.

There are more Letters from Germany in "Reflections of Guernsey".

Regina Krauer shows where the Channel Island's are situated and talks of the German Occupation

Dinner for One

Thank you Freddie Frinton! (and Hilmar & Regina!) 31st May 2012

I have just returned from a wonderful 15 day holiday in Germany. It was a very special time which I shall always remember for the wonderful green country, the cleanliness and the magnificent buildings, but mainly for the great friendliness and generosity of the people.

Let me explain. Hilmar and Regina invited me to their home in Marburg for a holiday. They had first spent a holiday in Guernsey in 1996 and 1997 and Hilmar especially loves books and he bought my book 'A Child's War'. He read it when they arrived home and was surprised to see a photograph of the TV star Freddie Frinton towards the back of the book.

When Hilmar and Regina decided on another holiday to Guernsey in 2000, Hilmar said he wanted to contact me and asked if he could call at our home, and I looked forward to meet this German couple as I had also met some very nice German people who had previously stayed at our 'Woodcote' guest house.

When they arrived at the house, I was surprised to be met and given a very nice presentation gift. They were keen for me to open this box after our tea. There was a bottle of sherry and also a DVD of Freddie Frinton in the 12 minute sketch 'Dinner for One'. I did not realise when I originally wrote my first book in 1985, that Freddie and 'Dinner for One' was so well known all over Germany. Every 31st December it is shown every half hour on the main television channels. You mention 'Dinner for One' to any German, and they laugh and smile and love the sketch. Incidentally, it is shown in English and is so very popular.

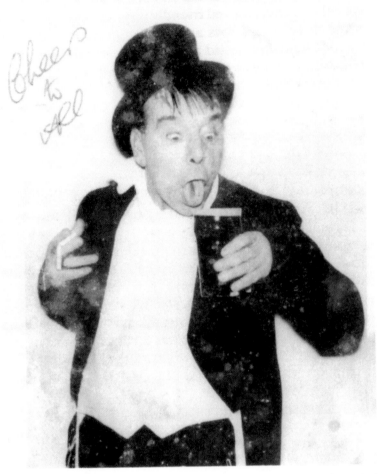

Hilmar and Regina never get tired of seeing it. They were so interested to know that Freddie had come to Guernsey with 'Stars in Battledress' to entertain the local population and British forces soon after our Liberation in 1945. We considered him, and others, as one of the Liberation heroes, and Freddie Frinton, like many others, came to our home and we enjoyed seeing him on stage at the Central Halls in the variety shows. I think we were privileged to have tickets.

Freddie knew we were in the audience, and would call to Mum ("Glad"), Joyce and I and we were naturally thrilled to hear him call our names, and to have a wave from him.

I had found Freddie's signed photograph amongst my mother's papers, so I decided to print it and to mention him often coming to our home. I well remember walking with him to the Little Chapel at Les Vauxbelets. After looking and showing off the Little Chapel to him, we sat on the grass and watched a farmer milking his cows. On offering us milk, we gladly accepted and enjoyed a bottle of lovely fresh milk from him. Little did I know then that through Freddie coming to our home, I would benefit 67 years later.

Hilmar and Regina made another short visit in 2002, and again in 2008, and we have kept in touch by writing letters, and always remembering Christmas and birthdays. When my 80th birthday loomed, I never dreamt I'd have such a wonderful present. With the card and letter came an invitation to their home in May 2012 for 10 days, with outings etc. at their expense. All I had to do was book a flight to Frankfurt and they would meet me at the airport. I could hardly believe what I was reading and they were also offering a trip on the River Rhine! That was somewhere I had always wanted to visit. I was hesitant at first. Ten days seemed a long time to leave the family, and for me to travel on my own. They must have been eager for my answer but being a little concerned, I did not answer straight away. They then wrote a lovely letter again, really wanting me to go and planned something every day for me, and also adding 4 days in Dresden (5-6 hours drive away to the east) making 15 days in all.

I accepted at last their invitation and we arranged that I would leave on May 16th 2012 (after the annual Liberation celebrations) and I would return on May 31st.

During the holiday, I was invited to read to students from my book at the Vocational College in Marburg where Regina teaches English and Spanish. The 50 students all spoke English and were very interested in the Occupation. The students' nationalities were German, French, Italian, Dominican Republic, Russian, Kazakh, Ukrainian, Moroccan, Congolese, Turkish, and Afghan. So many wanted to ask questions afterwards.

This was quite an experience for me and Regina and the director certainly made a big effort to put Guernsey on the map, placing a big screen showing Guernsey scenes, flags and Guernsey tea towels were hanging all around the large room. I was grateful to Malcolm Woodland for providing the resources, and for Occupation photographs, maps and details.

I also enjoyed a three hour cruise on the River Rhine and a trip on a paddle steamer on the River Elbe, and a motor boat on the Lake Edersee. Everything was planned, with not so much rush, but every day there was somewhere of interest to go. We also went to a symphony concert, and in Dresden there was a wonderful opera outing at the famous Semper Opera House. The four days in Dresden were planned to celebrate a friend and neighbour of Hilmar and Regina's, Karin's 70th birthday. There was a family get-together, we all enjoyed a coach trip and walking tour through the city, and stayed in a Farm Hotel which was lovely. I was totally spoilt by my hosts and everyone I met. Even after I returned home, I received an album full of lovely photographs by post, with the holiday itinerary. And all this through knowing Freddie Frinton for such a short time in 1945!

Unfortunately, I cannot thank Freddie Frinton for such a wonderful holiday as he died many years ago after keeping in touch with my mother and father for years. Unfortunately too, the letters from him were never kept.

My mother and father kept in touch with Freddie by letter, and it was his daughter who wrote to them saying he had died. Although in many films and television shows with Thora Hird, he was never as popular in the UK as he was in Australia, Finland, Sweden, Belgium, Norway, Denmark and of course Germany. In 'Dinner for One' he played the role of a butler who has to toast in the elderly lady on the occasion of her 90th birthday. In this role, he substitutes for four departed friends, emptying their glasses during each dinner course, thus getting gradually more and more drunk. He apparently never drank alcohol in real life. During the 1950s and 1960s he was a well known character comedian, and many may remember him co-starring with Thora Hird in the television series "Meet the Wife".

He was born on 17 January 1911 as Frederick Bitterner Coo in Grimsby. He was brought up by foster parents, married twice and had a family. Sadly, he suffered a heart attack at a young age and died on October 16th 1968.

Looking Back

On reflection, and remembering my dear mother and dear father's words, we were very grateful to have come through quite well and, having remained together, we were still a very close family. Despite all the worry, hard work and tension, not once during the five years had I seen my mother down. Worried and frightened, yes, but she was always cheerful, never any different. She really did not have much time to be miserable with up to nine in the family to keep happy and to feed, she just had to keep going. My mother's job was to queue and to cook, my father's evening job every night if lucky was cutting vegetables into cubes for the next day's soup. My father's help and love was my mother's comfort, and his support was always within reach. They had a wonderful happy marriage together.

Another consolation Mum and Dad had and were grateful for, and thankful my sister and I had not evacuated, was at least Mum and Dad did know where we were, how we were and what we were doing (at times!) We helped the food ration and the heating in our own small way and also helped by bringing home our young friends. Many a time I would play the piano with Mum and have a sing-song. There was no order against this and it all helped the time pass by. Mum and Dad were grateful too that at the end we were all together and grateful that all the family had been born and had been allowed to stay in Guernsey.

We often thought of friends who were interned in German Prison Camps. There were many people who were made to leave the island and amongst them English-born friends of my mother and father. After they left very suddenly, we had no more news of them and I remember very well Mum and Dad being very concerned. I often thought of my old friends too as going to Germany seemed like going to the end of the world to me then.

My childhood days were certainly different and all these experiences I remember very well.

I have never forgotten the happy school days at Vauvert and at the Occupation Intermediate School. I shall never forget the many happy hours and fun we had with Joyce Ferguson and with friends at Tap Dancing classes.

Ebenezer Church holds pleasant memories too. The Germans did not stop islanders attending church. Everyone was friendly and in the same boat, so to speak, and all made the most out of life.

Although I was young throughout, at no time did I feel nervous or frightened to leave the house. I used to take charge of my sister and our pram and off we would go. I think that if we had been stopped going on our little jaunts, Joyce and I would have been upset. Obviously we were very proud with our efforts to lessen the German ration and naturally had to keep our game a big secret! I am sure it was only our young and innocent looks that helped us get away with everything! It must have been the Mums and Dads of Guernsey who were the most worried and anxious at this difficult time for the safety and wellbeing of their families. Many Dads also were very worried as they were separated from their wives and children, those from whom they seldom heard as the Red Cross messages were very few and far between, they just lived to be reunited once again.

As my husband and I had a guest-house for almost 40 years and together with Mum and Dad we met many people who wanted to know about our Occupation, and I just had to tell our story. I do hope you have found the reading interesting and have enjoyed hearing of the family 'goings on'. My mother was certainly a character telling these stories and everyone would have a laugh, usually with the gathering of guests at Number 30, despite the worrying times that she and Dad had gone through. Freedom was wonderful for everyone.

My father died in 1972 aged 68, and my mother died aged 86 in 1991. She had been cheerful throughout her life. Following being widowed, Mum lived with my husband and I at 'Woodcote', Les Canichers, St Peter Port for many years.

My husband sadly died in 2010 and we have 2 married daughters, Sally Howlett and Carol Vivyan, both living in Guernsey with husbands Michael and Malcolm, and we have five grand-children, Ryan & Carly Howlett, Josh & Naomi Cottam and young Alice Rose (Rosie) Vivyan, all of whom we were both very proud. I have been grateful for our families' help, love and presence in writing this book. I feel now that I have completed my family memoirs and some of Guernsey's recent history.

It is over 70 years ago now. Thinking back to 1944 when our brave allied forces landed in France and when my dear mother had the most awful time worrying as to how she could feed the hungry family. I know if you have read my first book "A Child's War" you will have judged my mother to be quite a character. Everyone loved her – she was always full of fun and helped everyone she could, even through the worrying times, and she was a tonic to all who met her. What a story she could have written and what recipes she would have concocted out of what she could buy. Pity we hadn't kept the pram, the old faithful - it could have been famous in a museum, but Number 30 Rose Villa still remains and it will always be a very special place, if only it could speak and tell the tales! What an interesting and great story we would have, I am so very grateful to have been part of it, and especially so with the family I had. I have been, and still am, a very lucky lady.

Now, more than 68 years after the Liberation, may our children, grandchildren and future great grandchildren be blessed always with continued Peace and Freedom.

Mum & Dad in the
late 1940s at
Number 30 'Rose Villa'
Les Canichers.

Photograph
from Yvonne Fisher
and her Grandfather.

First published 2014 by Molly Bihet

Printed by: **Printed**, *La Garenne Park, Rue a Chiens, Vale, Guernsey GY6 8NX*

Page 142: Probably the only photo taken on 8 May 1945 with German soldiers freely walking around. It was a very special announcement and never to be forgotten. I took this photograph in Les Canichers of family, friends and neighbours after hearing Winston Churchill's broadcast: "Our dear Channel Islands will be free today". My mother is centre front with a rosette, Dad at the back with a flag, and Grandpa on the far left.

Foreward to A Child's War

It gives me great pleasure to write this foreword to A Child's War by Molly Bihet.

I have known Molly all her life and her mother, all my life. I have then read this book with the greatest interest. In writing the book, Molly has rendered a great service to our island and to prosperity by placing on record the fateful years of the German Occupation as seen through the extremely perspective and extremely penetrating eyes of a very young and typical Guernsey school girl.

The Occupation years were long, bitter and agonising. We all lived on a knife edge, not knowing from day to day what next would happen and always in danger and appalling difficulties in the long struggle for the very survival of the life of our community.

The Occupation did result in one great and inestimable blessing. In adversity may be, but it drew our people more closely together than ever before, and knitted them into one large and united family. It was a family which resisted to the fullest extent possible that Occupation and a family burning as ever with the fiercest pride of patriotism and of their Island and its heritage which the Occupation could never hope to weaken.

All this Molly brings out so clearly and so movingly in her book which should have a place of honour in the homes of all Guernsey men and Guernsey women.

Sir John Loveridge, Kt., C.B.E.
Bailiff of Guernsey 1973 to 1982
May 1985

I have chosen a few sentences from the many letters received over the years.

Reviews for A Child's War

A reader from Wales: "What a wonderful book, and what an achievement Molly. I laughed and I cried, it is really and truly lovely."

Mrs T from West Midlands: "Your book brought tears to my eyes - it was lovely".

Mrs R from Hampshire: ""We have all been fascinated by your account of life during the years of occupation, and the courage and humour with which you and your family and everyone faced the struggle to exist. The joy of freedom after victory and the hard work that went into recovery made heart-warming reading. Thank you ever so much".

Mr C from Twickenham: "I thoroughly enjoyed your book A Child's War, and I can see why it's been so successful! I loved some of the details, such as the sound made by the hose-pipe tyres on the bicycles: k-clump, k-clump; that's the sort of thing you don't often read about in books about the war! I also loved the pictures of you and Joyce performing as The Finigan Sisters, it must have given people a real boost to have entertainment like that".

Miss L from Australia: "Thank you very much for your book, I have thoroughly enjoyed it, and it brought back many memories".

Sharon from Worcester: "In our English lesson at school we have been reading your book A Child's War. I am writing to you to say how much I enjoyed it and I hope many more people enjoy your book as much as I did. The part of the book I most enjoyed was when Stan Workman played There'll Always Be An England and then God Save The King on the piano while several German soldiers were sitting in the front row of the concert hall. I also liked the bit when your family discovered that Pop Collins (your Granddad) had kept a gun after the Germans had ordered them to be handed in. I laughed at how you managed to acquire food by collecting potatoes in baskets, and scrounging some cement and carry it home in a pram".

Amy (age 8) from Hull: "I really enjoyed the book A Child's War. My best bit was when you and Joyce went looking for things like potatoes and wood".

A teacher from Bristol: "Your book A Child's War was very interesting and the children at my school were quite fascinated by it."

Mrs U from Essex: "I am writing to say how much I enjoyed your book A Child's War. How brave your parents were and how afraid they must all have been for you all. Otto was a nasty man wasn't he, but it was lovely to read of the German who wished to return your photographs. Your family had great strength. How lovely that you wrote to Winston Churchill and that you received a reply. It was a lovely book to read. I'm only sorry writing is not my best things and I am unable to express my thoughts to you. Thank you very much for a lovely book."

Mr & Mrs P from West Midlands: "What a marvellous insight you have given us. I have found your book most interesting. Thank you once again."

Rachel (age 13) from Essex: "I enjoyed your book very much and it made me realise all the things that happened during the German Occupation of Guernsey. The part which I enjoyed hearing about the most was when you and your sister went potato collecting. It must have been very frightening when Otto caught you and chased you down the road.

The food sounded very unappetising and it must have been such a relief when the Red Cross parcels came through, and another good part was when a German officer tried to swap his binoculars for half a bar of chocolate. Also I liked the way you and your family used the pram to collect things which came in useful. A good part of the book was when Pop Collins kept his best gun and hid it in the barrel of sawdust and how the Germans kept searching your home. The crystal radio must have been really good to listen to until you got caught by a German officer and gave you a fright."

Mr R from Oldham: "I am writing to tell you how wonderful your book was. It is a fascinating insight into what children were going through under the Jackboot."

Mr M from Eastbourne: "Your book is a fascinating - if somewhat awesome - look at what life was like in those days".

R.M. BBC Blue Peter Producer: "We could have listened to your wonderful stories all week. I'd enjoyed "A Child's War" and the sequel was perfect reading for our return flight."

K from France: "I've just finished reading "A Time for Memories". A lovely book, full of stories of real people, living a real war. Your three books have certainly filled me in about the lives of Guernsey folk 1940-45."

A.M. from Devon: "I am writing to say how much I enjoyed reading "A Child's War". It is a fascinating account of your life on Guernsey during the Occupation of the Channel Islands."

W.B. from High Wycombe: "My husband and I came to see you talk at Candie Gardens last Sunday 25 September. We have been reading your books for many years and were thrilled to have the opportunity to be so close to you and to hear first hand how your life, and that of others was, under the German Occupation."

L.K. from Canada: "I enjoyed your book immensely."

G.S. from Cheshire: "Thank you for sending me your book "Reflections of Guernsey". I can't tell you much I've enjoyed it – a marvellous story. My father ordered it for me as a surprise! Yes Molly, I also enjoyed your book "A Child's War".

M.H. from Cheshire: "I am writing to let you know how much I've enjoyed reading all three of your books."

R.P. from Birmingham: "I have just finished reading "A Child's War" and found it was a remarkable account of life under German Occupation. I loved the photograph of your mum. She must have been wonderful lady to cope with so many of you under those dark days."

Beatrice (age 11) from Guernsey: "Thank you very much for coming to our Liberation assembly at school. Your story was very interesting and everyone enjoyed it."

D. S. from the Isle of Wight: "Thank you so very much for the copy of "A Time for Memories". Many congratulations on another splendid book. I am sure it will be a great success.